The World of Gainsborough

TIME LIFE BOOKS ®

LIFE WORLD LIBRARY

LIFE NATURE LIBRARY

TIME READING PROGRAM

THE LIFE HISTORY OF THE UNITED STATES

LIFE SCIENCE LIBRARY

GREAT AGES OF MAN

TIME-LIFE LIBRARY OF ART

TIME-LIFE LIBRARY OF AMERICA

FOODS OF THE WORLD

THIS FABULOUS CENTURY

LIFE LIBRARY OF PHOTOGRAPHY

THE TIME-LIFE ENCYCLOPEDIA OF GARDENING

THE AMERICAN WILDERNESS

THE EMERGENCE OF MAN

THE OLD WEST

FAMILY LIBRARY:

    THE TIME-LIFE BOOK OF FAMILY FINANCE

    THE TIME-LIFE FAMILY LEGAL GUIDE

TIME-LIFE LIBRARY OF ART

The World of Gainsborough

1727-1788

by Jonathan Norton Leonard
and
the Editors of TIME-LIFE BOOKS

TIME-LIFE BOOKS, New York

About the Author

Jonathan Norton Leonard had a distinguished career as a freelance writer before joining TIME magazine, which he served as editor of the sections on Latin America and science. Among the books he has written for TIME-LIFE BOOKS are *Planets, Ancient America, Latin American Cooking, Early Japan, American Cooking: New England* and *American Cooking: The Great West.* Long interested in art and especially enchanted with the work of Gainsborough, Mr. Leonard traveled to England as special preparation for this book. He visited all the places where the artist had lived, studied most of the Gainsboroughs on public display, and was a guest in several castles and country mansions where Gainsborough portraits still hang in their original settings.

The Consulting Editor

H. W. Janson is Professor of Fine Arts at New York University, where he is also Chairman of the Department of Fine Arts at Washington Square College. Among his numerous publications are his *History of Art* and *The Sculpture of Donatello.*

The Consultant for This Book

Gert Schiff is Associate Professor of Fine Arts at New York University, Washington Square College. A specialist in English and German art of the 17th to 19th Centuries, Dr. Schiff received his Ph.D. in 1957 from Cologne University. Among his publications are a monograph on John Henry Fuseli (1741-1825), Swiss-born master of fantasy and nightmare, and the *catalogue raisonné* of Fuseli's works.

On the Slipcase

This radiant visage is that of Elizabeth Sheridan, wife of the brilliant playwright-Parliamentarian Richard Brinsley Sheridan and one of the great beauties of her day. Gainsborough's painting from which this detail is taken is shown on page 138.

End Papers

Front and Back: Deft and spontaneous, these black chalk landscape drawings by Gainsborough are two among hundreds the artist executed during his lifetime but never sold. They were made sometimes from memory and sometimes on the spot, partly as loosening-up exercises for the pastoral scenes that Gainsborough liked most to paint. (The Pierpont Morgan Library, New York.)

The following individuals and departments of Time Inc. were helpful in the production of this book: Editorial Production, Norman Airey, Nicholas Costino Jr.; Library, Benjamin Lightman; Picture Collection, Doris O'Neil; Photographic Laboratory, George Karas; TIME-LIFE News Service, Murray J. Gart; Correspondents Margot Hapgood and Rosemary Young (London) and Eleanor Hoover (Los Angeles).

Contents

I

An Apprentice in Rowdy London

Before the start of the 18th Century the damp island across the English Channel looked to the rest of Europe like a rather crude and violent land given more to bloodshed and turmoil than to art and culture. For decades the British had fought one another. They overthrew the autocratic King Charles I and chopped off his head, a horrible sacrilege in an age when kings were held to be agents of God. They set up a grim Puritan republic ruled by the commoner Oliver Cromwell, overthrew it in its turn and then drove another autocrat, James II, from his lawful throne.

In spite of political instability, the British had produced remarkable literature, and a few of their men of learning had won high reputations at home and abroad. But in the dominant art of painting, by which Continental Europeans tended to measure cultural achievement, the British lagged far behind. A few of their portraitists—notably the early 17th Century painter William Dobson—reached more than routine proficiency, but they were rare exceptions. British aristocrats usually employed foreign artists to paint their portraits and bought Italian or Dutch pictures to brighten their town and country houses. They seldom admired British paintings, and perhaps as a consequence of this lack of encouragement no native-born British artist had ever approached first rank.

But in the early 1700s Britain was on the threshold of a golden age. The Glorious Revolution of 1668, which ended the reign of James II, set William and Mary solidly on the throne, and prosperity rewarded domestic peace. Under a constitutional monarchy Britain's power expanded across all the oceans, London replaced Amsterdam as Europe's leading trade center, where goods from the ends of the earth were imported and redistributed to foreign buyers. London merchants grew monstrously rich, and the haughty landowning dukes and earls who dominated the government grew even richer. Towns and cities increased in size, creating a vigorous middle class. Even the laboring class shared considerably in the general well-being.

The same golden era that brought unprecedented prosperity to Britain was also a time of cultural growth. Manners and education improved, and so did the proficiency and status of British painters. By the end of the 18th Century, British noblemen and wealthy commoners no longer felt so strongly constrained to look abroad to fill their artistic needs, for with remarkable suddenness their own country had produced a number of great and near-great painters to rival the Continental masters. In little more than two generations a national school of painting had developed and reached maturity, and such names as William Hogarth, Allan Ramsay, Thomas Gainsborough, George Romney and Sir Joshua Reynolds had created works worthy of rank among the most brilliant in Europe.

Three of these—Hogarth, Gainsborough and Reynolds—had the touch of true genius. Hogarth, who came first by nearly a generation, was never a direct rival of the other two. Although he painted excellent portraits, he was a middle-class moralist and social reformer who gained fame for his earthy paintings and engravings that satirized the roistering life of 18th Century London. Gainsborough and Reynolds, later contemporaries, were in direct competition as fashionable portrait painters, but they could hardly have been more different from each other and from Hogarth. Gainsborough was easygoing, convivial, careless with his money. Reynolds, on the other hand, was a calculating artist-politician who cultivated aristocratic friends in order to achieve his lifelong ambition of raising the social standing of British artists.

Surely the most delightful of these great British painters was Thomas Gainsborough. He was born in 1727, soon after the start of Britain's age of national euphoria. His father, John Gainsborough, was a "clothier," a manufacturer and seller of cloth in the quiet Suffolk town of Sudbury, about 50 miles northeast of London, where his ancestors had been respectable burghers for at least 200 years. In those days the manufacture of cloth required no formal factory; it was largely a matter of supplying wool to cottage women who spun it into thread, and then having the thread woven into cloth on hand looms. Some of the weavers must have worked in John Gainsborough's house, for his famous son remarked years later: "Old pimply-nosed Rembrandt [he was thinking of Rembrandt's candid self-portraits] and myself were both born in a mill."

The "mill" was an ancient building that had once been an inn, The Black Horse, and was large enough to accommodate the looms and John Gainsborough's nine children, of whom Tom was the fifth son. It still stands though its original Tudor-style front, with its overhanging second story, has been replaced by a flat face of sober brick. It is now a museum devoted chiefly to the display of pictures by Sudbury's most renowned son. Across the street—now Gainsborough Street—is the Gainsborough Bookstore. There is also in Sudbury a Gainsborough pharmacy, a Gainsborough dry cleaner, a Gainsborough movie theater, hotel, guesthouse, petroleum company, a Gainsborough silk-weaving establishment, and the Gainsborough Labor and Social Club, which convivial Tom Gainsborough would doubtless appreciate if he were living today. A bronze statue of him with palette and brushes overlooks the market square, and filling stations in the vicinity advertise Gainsborough petrol with palette-shaped signs.

The boy who is modern Sudbury's hero came from an unusually interesting family. Though his father was hardly a gentleman by the

Gainsborough was born in the village of Sudbury, in Suffolk county, in the house at the center of the drawing above. The year was 1727 and Sudbury was a tranquil town set in a region whose gently rolling, luxuriantly wooded landscape was made famous in paintings first by young Tom and later by John Constable. A center for the wool trade, the area was a lifelong source of inspiration to Gainsborough, who once said, "Suffolk made me an artist."

definition of the time, he often dressed like one, took fencing lessons and wore a sword. He traveled on business to France and the Netherlands, and it is more than likely that he brought back reports of the artistic excitement he found there. Tom's mother was a cultivated woman whose avocation was painting pictures of flowers. His oldest brother, John, was an impractical inventor who spent his long life chasing mechanical will-o'-the-wisps; he made metal wings with which he attempted to fly, constructed a self-rocking cradle and designed "a cuckoo that sang all the year around." Another brother, Humphry, a dissenting (non-Church of England) clergyman, was a more sensible inventor. Among other achievements he seems to have come close to anticipating James Watt in the invention of a practical steam engine. It was just such a family, combining enterprise, intelligence and cultivation with a dash of eccentricity, that might be expected to include a genius.

There are plenty of stories about Tom Gainsborough's lighthearted boyhood, and some of them forecast his character in later life. He was not an eager scholar. When sent to the grammar school run by his mother's brother, the Reverend Humphry Burroughs, he spent much of his time drawing pictures for classmates, who paid for them by doing his lessons for him. During his free time he tramped the countryside, sketching on odd scraps of paper picturesque buildings, farm animals, plowmen and trees he especially loved.

There are legends that make him an accomplished painter in oils while still in grammar school; these are to be doubted, but his talents were certainly enough to convince his father that he could make a living as an artist of some sort. So when Tom was 13 he escaped further book learning and was sent off to London to live in the household of a respectable silver engraver. Silversmiths of the time engraved elaborate pictorial coats of arms on their pieces of "plate," and apprenticeship in the trade was considered a good approach to an artistic vocation.

A generation or so earlier the elder Gainsborough might not have made this risky decision for his son, but in 1740, when Tom set out for London, the golden age of British painting had already begun. A strange, rambunctious, many-talented man, William Hogarth, had proved that a native-born British painter could make a good living and stir up as much artistic excitement as any Italian or Dutchman.

The London to which Tom traveled—by stagecoach, slow-moving passenger wagon, perhaps on foot—was Hogarth's London. His genius portrayed it in such minute detail that it lives vividly today in all its wealth and squalor, vigor and violence. It was a crowded, fast-growing city of over 600,000 people, already one of the biggest in Europe and often denounced as a cancer swelling at the cost of the rest of England. London was a powerhouse that attracted talent from everywhere and spread English ideas and the English language around the earth. It was Hogarth's London, with its promise of artistic fortune, that drew Tom Gainsborough into its stench and roar.

Hogarth was the son of an impoverished schoolteacher who made a precarious living by such literary drudgery as compiling dictionaries. Born in London in 1697, Hogarth hardly ever left the city that he criticized, satirized, preached at and loved. In 1712, when he was 15, he was apprenticed to a silver engraver, and his well-known example may have led John Gainsborough to do the same for his son 28 years later. Hogarth's first "works" were intricate decorations on silver tankards and platters, but as soon as he was free of apprenticeship he took up the more ambitious trade of engraving on copper for reproduction. With wonderful prolificacy he turned out pictorial advertising cards for shops, billheads and theater tickets. Then came book illustrations and scathing satirical engravings, which were sold in bookshops at a shilling per copy.

The first of these satiric works was a savage attack on the South Sea Company, a speculative venture that became known as the South Sea Bubble after it burst disastrously in 1720. The faces of some of the figures that fill the picture to overflowing and represent the company's directors and their victims are portraits of real celebrities; the hunchbacked pickpocket in the lower center was quickly identified by the public as the poet Alexander Pope, who is shown robbing the playwright John Gay. Libel laws of the early 18th Century were too flaccid to spoil such fun.

The South Sea Scheme (pages 18-19), engraved when Hogarth was 24, shows many characteristics that would mark his work throughout his career. Perhaps because of his upbringing in crowded London, where few people had rooms or even beds to themselves, he seemed loath to leave an inch of space unused. His designs are multiringed circuses packed with allegorical figures—Honor being flogged by Self-Interest, Truth beset by Villainy, Despair beckoned by Fraud. This type of engraving had its roots in the Netherlands, but Hogarth gave it unexampled vigor.

Always close to the surface of Hogarth the artist was Hogarth the preacher. He was indefatigably moral, with a strong strain of puritanism that sometimes yielded, as puritanism frequently will, to the temptation to titillate while denouncing sin. His favorite targets were the idle rich and women of less than impregnable virtue, many varieties of whom abounded in 18th Century London. He was also death on corrupt officials, Roman Catholics and all kinds of foreigners.

To dwell on Hogarth's preachiness, however, does him an injustice. Most of the evils that he attacked were very real ones. For example, his shocking engraving *Gin Lane (page 21),* which swarms with tattered drunkards, cripples and suicides, was aimed at the unregulated traffic in cheap spirits that was having a horrible effect on the English working class. Its companion picture, *Beer Street (page 20),* with its portly, well-dressed figures, showed the happy prosperity that came from drinking nothing stronger than honest British beer. But Hogarth was more than just a preacher; while painting his pictorial sermons he spent time, money and energy promoting and managing charitable institutions such as orphanages, foundling homes and hospitals. Seldom has a painter done so much to improve social conditions in his native city.

Hogarth's style, even in the midst of his most passionate sermons, was always wonderfully lively and interesting. He was also technically versatile, turning from engraving to painting with no trouble at all. His interest in becoming a painter had been stimulated by the works of Sir James Thornhill, an adept, fashionable and successful artist who held the high-

Hogarth issued this shop card to attract customers in 1720 when, aged 23, he set up on his own as an engraver. The figures at the sides represent Art *(left)* and History. In addition to such cards—used by many kinds of tradesmen as advertisements—Hogarth engraved bookplates, bills and letterheads. These routine commissions were his bread and butter for the next decade, while he made a reputation for the work he preferred: book illustrations and topical prints.

sounding title of Serjeant-Painter to the King. For a brief time Hogarth studied painting at an academy run by Thornhill. He may not have learned much from his teacher (he was soon painting better than Thornhill), but in 1729 he eloped with Thornhill's daughter. Forced to earn more money to support her without her father's help, he resorted to "conversation pieces," a popular type of painting recently imported from the Continent.

Most conversation pieces showed little conversation; they were small group portraits, usually of a family posed in its stiffest finery. Generally overcrowded, they had low artistic value, but they were a cheap way of getting several portraits for the price of one. However, the labor of turning out these bargain-basement portraits was considerable, and Hogarth abandoned them as soon as he could find another mode of painting that could afford a reliable income.

His new inspiration came from the theater. In 1728 John Gay's *The Beggar's Opera,* a lively musical drama about the London underworld of prostitutes, pimps and thieves, had swept the city as had no play within living memory. It enchanted Hogarth, a connoisseur of London in all its aspects, and he promptly painted and publicized a marvelous picture of one of its most arresting scenes—two lovely girls pleading for the life of their highwayman lover. The picture won much attention and helped to attract eager sitters for his multiple portraits.

Hogarth was always the businessman, and this quick success gave him a golden idea: instead of depicting lively scenes from another man's play, why not imagine scenes of his own suitable for picturing? His first attempt, in 1731, was a pair of paintings entitled *Before* and *After,* illustrating a seduction. Said to have been commissioned by "a certain vicious nobleman," the pictures nevertheless contain an element of moralizing in that the man in *After* looks somewhat dazed and unhappy despite his lustful conquest.

Hogarth listened to glowing comments on *Before* and *After* and saw in such pictures, which combined moralizing with titillation, a way to carry his preachings to the largest possible audience. Always and genuinely the moral man, he describes his motives as follows: "I therefore turned my thoughts to a still more novel mode, viz. painting modern moral subjects, a field not broken up [cultivated] in any country or any age. . . . In these compositions those subjects which will both entertain and improve the mind bid fair to be of the greatest utility and must therefore be entitled to rank in the highest class."

To put his plan into operation, Hogarth intended to paint a single picture dramatizing woman's fall, with enough titillation to insure its popularity. Before he completed his project he had multiplied one painting into a series of six. *A Harlot's Progress* delighted all classes of London's population and won its creator a unique and permanent place in the history of art. The paintings themselves were destroyed in a fire in 1755, but excellent engravings—which Hogarth sold in advance by subscription and with much loud publicity—reveal the intimate detail of the originals. In the first picture of the series a poor, pretty and demure young country girl, Moll Hackabout, arrives in London in search of honest employment. The picture teems with tear-jerking sentiment: the girl wears

After he ended his apprenticeship to a silversmith and went into business for himself, Hogarth could afford to abandon the drudgery of creating fancy crests for tableware. But he made an exception for an artists' club he belonged to and engraved this elaborate design on the tankard shown below. The club members' interests are symbolized by the painter, sculptor and musical instruments grouped around a vaguely Biblical scene. Though posed in a fanciful baroque setting, the two large figures are drawn with a realism foreshadowing the style that Hogarth would later use in his famous satires.

a rose at her breast, symbolizing innocence, and has brought a goose in a basket to give to some worthy relative. Her old father, a threadbare clergyman, has come with her to the wicked city with a letter of introduction to a bishop. The letter does his daughter no good. Moll falls into the evil hands of a brothel keeper, and in subsequent pictures she sinks lower and lower as a prostitute and finally dies of venereal disease. Her mourners are mostly prostitutes, one of whom serves gin on the coffin. The parson who officiates has his hand under a young woman's skirt, and the undertaker is dallying with another, whose breast has already popped out of her bodice.

This highly moral series with unmoral embellishments was the toast of Londoners, who joyfully identified its characters as real people. When the third engraving of the series appeared, the news reached a meeting of the Board of Treasury that poor Moll had been arrested by Sir John Gonson, a magistrate famous for his one-man war on prostitutes; the noble lords adjourned and each rushed out to buy his own copy. Whether or not *A Harlot's Progress* improved the minds of its admirers, as its creator intended, Hogarth's fame was assured. But he did not profit financially as much as he had hoped. The pictures were immediately pirated, and engraved copies of varying quality were sold in enormous numbers with no benefit to the original artist—a situation that was common at the time. Hogarth reacted with characteristic vigor; he got influential friends to pressure Parliament until, in 1735, it passed a copyright law called "Hogarth's Act" protecting artists' rights in the reproductions of their works.

While lobbying in Parliament, Hogarth was hard at work painting his next moralizing series, *A Rake's Progress,* whose publication as engravings he held up until the copyright law was safely passed. Closely paralleling its predecessor, this series shows the mounting troubles of a foolish young fop who inherits the fortune of his miserly father and attempts to keep up with the gaudy and licentious aristocrats who lead London society. His money eventually runs out and he tries to recoup his fortune by marrying a rich, elderly, one-eyed woman. Even this does not suffice. The Rake is thrown into debtor's prison and finally dies in an insane asylum.

A Rake's Progress, its engraved reproductions protected by Hogarth's Act, earned Hogarth a great deal of money and permitted him to give attention to his lifelong ambition, which was to paint "history pictures." Such paintings were considered the peak of artistic achievement. They were the continuance of a long tradition that had started many centuries earlier with the painting of Bible stories and the lives of saints for the Church. Later, when kings usurped the supreme power of the Church and assumed some of its divinity, history paintings were commissioned to glorify royal virtues and victories. But British artists were never good at works of this sort, and by Hogarth's time the tradition was no longer strong. Nevertheless, he spent the better part of two years painting two enormous pictures on Biblical themes—*The Pool of Bethesda* and *The Good Samaritan.* Unfortunately, the paintings showed none of Hogarth's usual vigor or spontaneity. They were obviously done in imitation of various old masters, whose works Hogarth had carefully studied in spite of

A proud member of England's emerging middle class, Hogarth portrayed himself with unabashed candor in 1745, when he was at the peak of his career. His snub-featured face, with a scar from a childhood accident on his forehead, reveals the determined assertiveness appropriate to a self-made man. His palette, adorned with a sinuous line—his famous "Line of Beauty" —lies beside books by his favorite authors —Shakespeare, Milton and Swift. And he gave as much space to his boon companion Trump, the pug dog, as to himself.

his often-expressed disapproval of foreign painters. The paintings earned him little praise and no commissions.

After this reverse Hogarth reluctantly and temporarily abandoned history painting. To recoup his fortunes he returned to the satiric paintings that he did so wonderfully well. After the death of his father-in-law, Sir James Thornhill, he also reorganized Thornhill's art academy where he had once studied. Under new management it continued to operate until the Royal Academy, with its associated art schools, was founded in 1768. Hogarth was now a leading citizen of London, and although some of his patrons were highborn he made no effort to attach himself socially to the aristocracy, as so many successful commoners did. Instead, he remained proudly a member of the city's solid, powerful middle class, busy with charitable works and concerned about the virtue of all classes.

Having reached a respectable social position, Hogarth turned to life-sized portrait painting, a traditional road to artistic prosperity and one that he had not tried before. His first serious production was a full-length portrait of Captain Thomas Coram, a prominent philanthropist, shipbuilder and self-made man. Hogarth proclaimed in advance that the picture would challenge the tradition of Van Dyck's elegant portraits of English aristocrats of the previous century, and would prove that a native-born British painter could do as well for a middle-class sitter. *Captain Coram (page 35)* accomplished both those things. It was a great artistic success and is certainly one of the best portraits ever painted in England. Its background and foreground symbolize the sea, where the good captain won his fortune, and the face of the subject glows with virtues that Hogarth admired: intelligence, good humor, honesty and morality. The captain must have been mightily pleased, as are most people who look at his portrait today.

Hogarth painted other life-sized portraits, including a few of the Royal Family, but at this kind of work he was not a commercial success. One of the reasons—perhaps the controlling one—is not hard to see. His brush never lacked magic, but his preoccupation with middle-class morality got in its way. To almost all his sitters he gave the same smug, righteous, plain, honest look that can fairly be called Hogarth's "look of virtue." He awarded it to himself in his self-portraits and to women, including a duchess. Even children, even his dog, got some of this virtuous look. But not many noble patrons, the richest source of portrait money, and certainly few of their elegant women, wanted to look that homely way. So Hogarth never became a fashionable portrait painter.

H e could, when he chose, paint extremely pretty women, but the puritanical preacher dwelling inside him seems to have associated feminine attractiveness with vice, or at least with sin. The prostitutes who abound in his moralizing pictures are young, comely and seldom evil-looking. Actresses, whose profession was far from respectable in 18th Century London, are also delightfully portrayed, and so is the girl who struggles and yields in *Before* and *After*. Even in a horrifying picture called *Satan, Sin and Death*, the central figure, Sin, is a naked, beautiful woman. The faces of most of these symbolic figures look much alike; they have Hogarth's attractive but disapproving "look of sin." If he could be asked

Satirist Hogarth was himself often satirized. This lampoon by Paul Sandby, an artist associated with an anti-Hogarth clique, ridiculed what his enemies considered his ignorance of artistic tradition. Hogarth, in the guise of his own pet pug, sits at his easel painting a ludicrously contemporary version of Abraham sacrificing Isaac—the Old Testament patriarch shoots his son with an 18th Century musket. A butterfly (a symbol of vanity) perched on his shoulder and a foppish admirer at his elbow urge the artist on. Hogarth, the cartoon implies, is as oblivious of the example of the old masters as he is of the racket made by his oafish assistants *(background)* and barking dogs.

why he made his female sinners so pretty, he would undoubtedly answer, like many another preacher, that sin is indeed attractive and therefore all the more dangerous, and so it should be shown with all its treacherous charm.

Almost as if to prove that he could show women who were pretty as well as nonsinful, Hogarth painted late in his career his charming *Shrimp Girl.* It is not a finished portrait, hardly more than a rapid sketch to preserve an impression, but it lights up the space around it with gaiety and innocence. It was not meant for sale and shows that this glorious painter, who could do anything, could happily free himself on occasion from the compulsion to paint with a purpose.

In 1743, while still doing a few portraits, Hogarth began work on his most brilliant achievement, the series called *Marriage à la Mode (pages 29-31).* In this he combined his moralizing with a subtlety and economy of design not apparent in most of his other satiric works. He intended to have the series of six engraved for reproduction, but he also hoped to sell the paintings themselves for high prices. Therefore he painted them all with meticulous care, which was not always the case with earlier works of his that were headed for the engraver's tool.

Marriage à la Mode is the story of the loveless marriage of the dissolute son of a nobleman and the frivolous daughter of a rich but stingy commoner. The ending is what might be expected: the young earl is killed by his wife's lover, who escapes out the window in his nightshirt; in the last picture the wife returns to her father's dingy home and, disillusioned with life, takes poison. Included in the story are characteristic Hogarth titillations, subtly handled but many of them still so earthy that they are seldom described in print.

Marriage à la Mode made Hogarth a small fortune, and at the same time his other engravings sold excellently. He could afford a comfortable London town house and a country villa in nearby Chiswick, preserved today as a Hogarth museum. He kept six servants and painted their portraits affectionately on a single canvas *(page 34),* giving them all a gentle touch of his approving "look of virtue."

However, in his later years Hogarth was not a happy man. One reason was the reaction to his book, *The Analysis of Beauty,* which he published in 1753. The book is partly an elaborate theory of esthetics based on the idea that those things that evoke a feeling of great pleasure are expressed in curved, serpentine lines—Hogarth's well-known "Line of Beauty." Partly it is an appeal to artists to get their ideas direct from nature, not from traditions of art. A few critics liked the book; most did not, and some of them derided Hogarth as a man of little education who was writing about philosophical matters far beyond his depth. Nor did his paintings—sometimes auctioned in his own house, where he limited bidding on each lot to exactly five minutes—bring the prices he felt they deserved. When he died in 1764, Hogarth had done little painting for more than 10 years.

Hogarth had been close to the peak of his fame when Tom Gainsborough arrived in London in 1740. The city Hogarth loved so well was bursting with vitality. A visitor from comparatively quiet Germany, the

Hogarth drew the serpentine lines of beard and hair in this sketch of a 17th Century portrait bust to illustrate the "Line of Beauty," a cardinal point in his theory of esthetics. Such graceful curves, he wrote in his book, *The Analysis of Beauty,* are essential to the most elegant art because their "varied play, twisting together in a flame-like manner," charms the eye.

physicist Professor Georg Christoph Lichtenberg, an enthusiastic commentator on Hogarth, wrote his impressions of it some years later: "On both sides of the street are tall houses with plate-glass windows. The lower floors consist of shops and seem to be made entirely of glass; many thousand candles light up silverware, engravings, books, clocks, glass, pewter, paintings, women's finery, modish and otherwise, gold, precious stones, steel-work, and endless coffee-rooms and lottery offices. The street looks as though it were illuminated for some festivity. . . . In the middle of the street roll chaises, carriages and drays in an unending stream. Above this din, and the hum and clatter of thousands of tongues and feet, one hears the chimes from church towers, the bells of the postmen, the organs, fiddles, hurdy-gurdies, and the tambourines of English mountebanks, and the cries of those who sell hot and cold viands in the open at the street-corners. Then you will see a bonfire of shavings flaring up as high as the upper stories of the houses in a circle of merrily shouting beggar boys, sailors and rogues. Suddenly a man whose handkerchief has been stolen will cry 'Stop Thief!' and everyone will begin running and pushing and shoving. . . . Before you know where you are, a pretty, nicely dressed miss will take you by the hand: 'Come, my lord, come along, let us drink a glass together . . .' Then there is an accident forty paces from you . . . but all of a sudden they are laughing again. . . . That is Cheapside and Fleet Street on a December evening."

The diversions that formed an integral part of the scene in 18th Century London were as boisterous as the city's workaday life. Spectacles of all kinds were enormously popular with all classes. These ranged from theatrical performances, displays of fireworks and fairs—with their "musick, showes, drinking, gaming, raffling, lotteries, stage-plays and drolls"—to such cruel sights as cockfights and bulls or bears being baited by dogs. Thousands flocked to see public executions, and it was considered amusing to visit the madhouse of Bedlam to observe the ravings of the inmates.

A number of amusement centers, one of the most famous of which was Vauxhall, or Spring Gardens, drew huge crowds. The masses came to gape at the antics and elaborate dress of the "ton," or fashionable portion of London's population; the aristocrats and well-to-do to attend balls, listen to concerts, and sip tea or eat ices while exchanging the latest scandal. During Hogarth's time, *England's Gazetteer* carried an account of some of Vauxhall's attractions: "This is the place where are those so-called Spring Gardens, laid out in so grand a taste that they are frequented in the three summer months by most of the nobility and gentry then in and near London. . . . Here are fine pavilions, shady groves, and most delightful walks, illuminated by about one thousand lamps, so disposed that they all take fire together, almost as quick as lightning, and cast such a sudden blaze as is perfectly surprising." The writer Horace Walpole, describing a visit to Vauxhall with a friend, tells of their difficulty in arriving there because the "tide and torrent of coaches was so prodigious. We then alighted, and after scrambling under the bellies of horses, through wheels and over posts and rails, we reached the gardens, where were already many thousand persons."

London's sights and uproar must have made quite an impression on 13-

year-old Tom Gainsborough from the tranquil town of Sudbury. But unlike Hogarth's poor country heroine Moll Hackabout, Tom was met by friends and taken safely to the house of the silver engraver to whom he was apprenticed.

Of his youthful years in London Gainsborough left little record. They are almost a blank, filled in here and there by shreds of evidence. He is known to have left the silversmith sometime before 1745 and gone to work for Hubert Gravelot, an excellent French pictorial engraver who was in London from 1732 to 1746. Gainsborough could have encountered no better influence. Gravelot knew everybody in London's artistic circles, and he kept in touch with France, whose pastoral paintings, with their dainty figures, were having a strong effect on British taste. To pay for his counsel, the young boy helped the Frenchman with his engraving work, being entrusted with more and more important parts of pictures as he improved.

There is no proof that Gainsborough ever met Hogarth, although it is believed that he spent a little time in the art school that Hogarth supervised. He is said to have done sculptural modeling before he turned to painting, and evidence of this is a plaster cast of an old, droopy horse modeled in clay which is preserved in the Gainsborough Museum in Sudbury. It looks like all the horses that Gainsborough—who sympathized with weary old horses—would put in his own landscapes for the rest of his life.

Gainsborough seems to have needed little formal training in painting; the necessary skills came naturally to him. As his proficiency increased, he was hired by art dealers to repair old paintings, and this work gave him a chance to study intimately the techniques of famous foreign artists. He was particularly impressed with the 17th Century Dutch landscape painters Jacob van Ruisdael and Jan Wynants, who were to have a deep influence on his own landscape work. In these various ways the talented boy earned a living; in later years one of his friends reported that Gainsborough had been no expense to his father after he left for London at the age of 13.

Of all the contemporary English artists, probably the one who influenced Gainsborough most was Francis Hayman, an almost first-rate painter and engraver who tried everything from theatrical scenery to historical painting and portraiture. He is best known for his lively scenes based on Shakespeare's plays, and for other large paintings that decorated the pavilion built for the Prince of Wales at Vauxhall. As a young man, Gainsborough worked in Hayman's London studio between periodic visits to Sudbury. It is thought that he painted the landscape backgrounds of some of Hayman's pictures. Certainly Hayman's way of painting conversation pieces left its mark on Gainsborough's early style.

Another kind of influence that Hayman may have had on Gainsborough is darkly hinted at by some biographers. Like a number of artists, Hayman did not lead an exemplary moral life. He spent much time in taverns and brothels and drank more than was good for him. He may have taught his young protégé some of these bad habits, but perhaps little urging was needed. In a letter Gainsborough later wrote to a friend, the

Gainsborough was 18 or 19 when he made this appealing clay model of a tuckered-out work horse. Later he seldom worked as a sculptor, but he continued to depict animals with perception and appreciation throughout his career: spirited hunting dogs appear in his portraits, comfortable household cats in his pictures of children and serene cattle in his landscapes.

GAINSBOROUGH'S HOUSE SOCIETY, SUDBURY

actor John Henderson, he noted that the streets of London were "my first school, and deeply read in petticoats I am." He certainly drank a good deal throughout his life and retained a keen interest in beautiful women. But the habits that his proper biographers suggest were learned from Hayman were not bad enough to handicap him. Neither drinking nor "petticoat reading" kept him from turning out, year after year, an extraordinary amount of first-class work.

Many other artists were busy in London in the 1740s, for the city's great prosperity both attracted and created them. Dutch, French and Italian painters, who swarmed across the Channel to serve rich British patrons, were met for the first time by worthy native-born rivals. The Scotsman Allan Ramsay, who had studied in Italy, was quite as good at portrait painting as any of the foreigners; he was, in fact, the first British painter, with the exception of Hogarth at his best, who could make a portrait a work of art instead of merely a decorative likeness. Ramsay usually made his sitters look rather austere, but his women could be beautiful too, and his men's features often showed an attractive, strong nobility.

It is not recorded that Gainsborough was taught by Ramsay, or even knew him, but he may have been influenced by the elegance of the older man's style, so different from that of the earthy, middle-class Hogarth. He could have also been inspired, in a practical way, by Ramsay's popularity with the moneyed aristocrats who commissioned portraits.

Even more successful than Ramsay, at least commercially, was Thomas Hudson, who ran a sort of portrait factory that turned out stiff, competent likenesses as if they were china plates. Hudson himself did little of the work, painting only certain parts of each picture—probably the faces—and doubtless keeping charge of the all-important sales department. For the clothing, draperies and backgrounds he employed a group of specialists. A sitter could choose from several standard poses and be sure that the finished portrait would be worthy of hanging among those of his ancestors.

For an intuitive artist like young Gainsborough, Hudson's prosperous but mechanical institution could have had little attraction. But if he had visited there when he was 16, either from curiosity or to earn a few shillings, he might have met an earnest, 20-year-old apprentice who would one day be his chief rival for honors as the greatest British painter of his day. Joshua Reynolds was a wholly different sort of person from Gainsborough. He had consciously planned his career and was making influential friends as fast as he could. He was not "deeply read in petticoats," and if he went to taverns it was to meet important men whom he hoped to find there. Where Gainsborough was a trifle raffish, Reynolds was proper; he was prudent rather than reckless and purposeful rather than intuitive. In 1743 he decided he had learned all he could in Hudson's portrait factory, so he returned to his home in Devonshire to try his own hand at portraits and to lay the foundations of his social career by cultivating aristocratic naval officers based in nearby Plymouth. Already Reynolds was beginning to inhabit a different sphere from Gainsborough, and there is no proof that they ever met until both men had won fame in the gorgeous world of London society.

Hogarth's Sinful City

While Gainsborough was still a boy, the Londoner William Hogarth was providing English art—and himself—with a good name. Hogarth was almost alone in arguing that native painters could match Europe's best. He derided the "shiploads of dead Christs, Madonnas and Holy Families" that were imported from the Continent by wealthy but uncritical English collectors. But his faith in the English artist was, in turn, ridiculed —and with some justice. Before Hogarth, English painters had been a soggy lot, awash in undistinguished portraits and "historical painting" based on Biblical and mythological themes and episodes from English history. Ironically, Hogarth himself aspired to be a "historical painter," but he found his fame, fortune and subject matter in England's lively present, not in its past. He attacked the hypocrisies of society with scathing satirical allegories like *The South Sea Scheme (right)*. And he invented his own picture "dramas" of people caught up in the turbulence of London's high—and low—life.

A superb painter, engraver and talented writer who often captioned his works, Hogarth had the common touch. His crusading zeal, ribald wit and themes of moral uplift sold countless numbers of his prints. His success did not lessen his combativeness—he battled for copyright laws and exhibition halls to raise the status of English artists. Eventually, Hogarth awoke his countrymen to the potentialities of home-grown art.

This early print by Hogarth was an allegorical attack on a wave of disastrous financial speculation that had just swept England. To help eliminate the national debt, the government had sponsored the

The South Sea Scheme, 1721

South Sea Company, which put investors' funds into such dubious projects as a gold mine in Spanish-ruled Peru. Corporate corruption was rife, and when the bubble burst it cost many people their savings, estates and honor. The center of Hogarth's print is a human wheel of fortune topped by a goat and the slogan "Who'l Ride." At left, a winged devil (A) with a scythe throws chunks of Fortune's body (B) to the grasping crowd. A Protestant, Catholic and Jew gamble (C) while Honesty (D) is broken on the wheel of Self-Interest (G) and Villainy (F) whips Honor (E). In the lower right-hand corner Trade lies dead.

19

BEER STREET.

Beer, happy Produce of our Isle
Can sinewy Strength impart,
And wearied with Fatigue and Toil
Can chear each manly Heart.

Labour and Art upheld by Thee
Successfully advance,
We quaff Thy balmy Juice with Glee
And Water leave to France.

Genius of Health, thy grateful Taste
Rivals the Cup of Jove,
And warms each English generous Breast
With Liberty and Love.

Publish'd according to Act of Parliament Feb.1.1751.

Beer Street, 1750-1751

In satirizing the faults of English society Hogarth never understated matters. He crammed his scenes with people enacting every conceivable—and some almost inconceivable—aspects of the case in hand. In the engravings above, Hogarth compares the joys of beer drinking with the ravages of gin. On Beer Street life is tranquil, the denizens compatible. The pawnshop is crumbling from disuse; chubby, contented burghers live within their means while enjoying the moderation of traditional English beer.

Gin Lane is the vicious opposite of Beer Street. A drunken mother lets her baby fall from her arms as she

20

GIN LANE.

Designd by W. Hogarth

Gin cursed Fiend, with Fury fraught,
Makes human Race a Prey,
It enters by a deadly Draught,
And steals our Life away.

Virtue and Truth, driv'n to Despair.
It's Rage compells to fly.
But cherishes, with hellish Care.
Theft, Murder, Perjury.

Damn'd Cup! that on the Vitals preys,
That liquid Fire contains,
Which Madness to the Heart conveys,
And rolls it thro' the Veins.

Publish'd according to Act of Parliamt Febry 1751

Gin Lane, 1750-1751

reaches for a pinch of snuff. The pawnbroker is besieged by tipplers desperately in need of money to buy liquor. Another mother, at right, pours gin into her baby's mouth to pacify him while around her the drinkers disport themselves like so many animals. In the background a barber has hanged himself because no one on Gin Lane has enough pride to care about personal grooming.

The print is a masterly collection of excesses, yet Hogarth was working well within the facts. Gin and other hard liquors were cheap and could be sold without license —distillers operated with government approval because they bought surplus grain, thus swelling farm income.

21

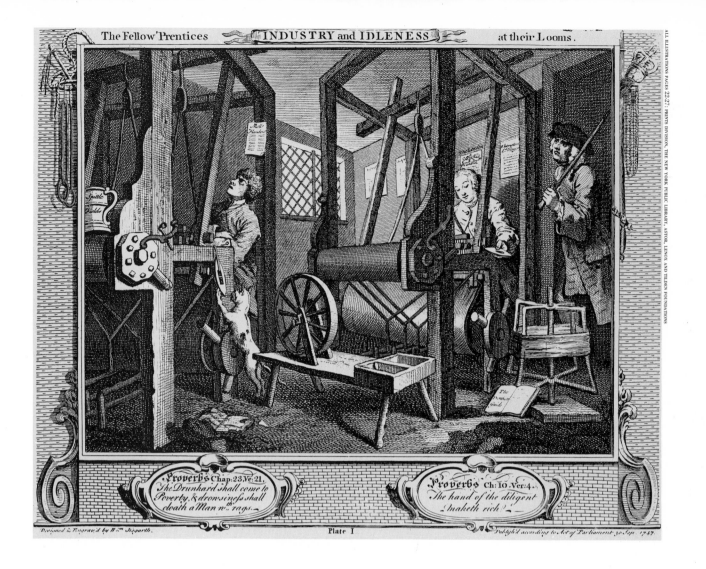

ALL ILLUSTRATIONS PAGES 22-27; PRINTS DIVISION, THE NEW YORK PUBLIC LIBRARY, ASTOR, LENOX AND TILDEN FOUNDATIONS

Proverbs Chap: 23 Ve: 21.
The Drunkard shall come to
Poverty, & drowsiness shall
cloath a Man w:th rags.

Proverbs Ch: 10 Ver: 4.
The hand of the diligent
maketh rich.

Designed & Engrav'd by W:m Hogarth.   Plate I   Publish'd according to Act of Parliament 30 Sep. 1747.

The Fates of Good and Bad Boys

Hogarth became the darling of the English public through cautionary tales in which he created his own plot, characters and moral enlightenment. In his autobiography he wrote: "I have endeavored to treat my subjects as a dramatic writer: my picture is my stage, and men and women my players, who, by means of certain actions and gestures, are to exhibit a dumb show." Relying on the facility of his brush, Hogarth usually painted a scene first, then made an engraving of it to supply the prints that invariably became bestsellers.

One of his most popular picture-dramas was *Industry and Idleness (this page through page 27),* a homily about the rewards of hard work and the wages of idleness. Simple as this moral seems, Hogarth was too much the realist to deal only in such absolute terms as right and wrong. His hero is the apprentice who does his job well, but he also has the wit to marry the boss's daughter and

the self-confidence to push himself into public life. The successful middle-class people with whom he associates are all too human in their comfort and satisfaction with the life of privilege they enjoy.

Hogarth contrasts his industrious hero with a lazy apprentice, a laggard who is content among the dregs of society. In this shoddy world, Hogarth's characters are a rowdy, zesty lot; he captures the coarse appeal of their wayward life with its easy pleasures, jungle code of ethics and quick betrayals. At the end of the drama, the hard-working apprentice sits in judgment of his idle counterpart. One has obviously done well, the other miserably. Yet the tale clearly shows that each is the product of the English society Hogarth observed and understood so well. As though to reinforce the moral message in his scenes, the artist added to each picture quotations from the Bible set in embellished frames.

The INDUSTRIOUS 'PRENTICE performing the Duty of a Christian.

Psalm CXIX Ver: 97.
O! How I love thy Law it is my meditation all the day

Plate 2

From the start, the idle
apprentice is up to no
good. He neglects his loom
at the weaver's workshop
(opposite page), has a
tankard of beer within
easy grasp and dozes
while a cat plays with his
shuttle. Tacked above his
head is a ballad about the
notorious lady of pleasure,
Moll Flanders; his copy of
"The Prentices Guide"
lies torn at his feet. His
master, outraged by such
behavior, stands in the
doorway shaking his stick
at the slovenly boy.
Meanwhile, the
industrious apprentice
works hard, studies "The
Prentices Guide" and
takes the boss's daughter
to church services (left).

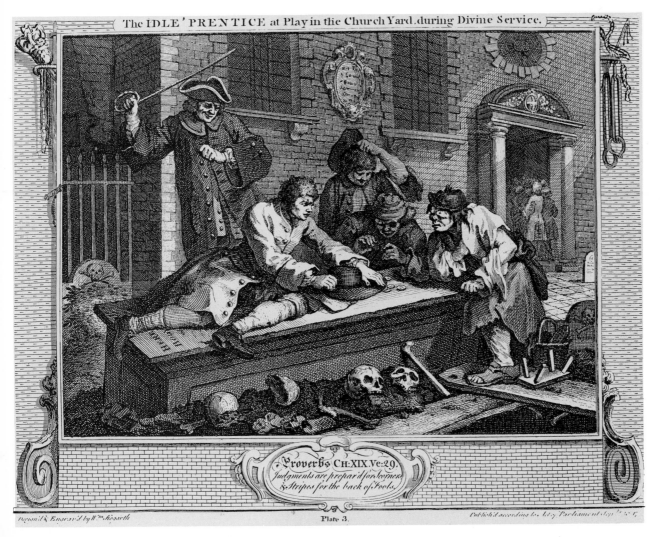

The IDLE 'PRENTICE at Play in the Church Yard during Divine Service.

Proverbs Ch: XIX. Ve: 29.
Judgments are prepar'd for Scorners
& Stripes for the back of Fools.

Plate 3.

Outside the church the
idle apprentice cheats at a
game called hustle-cap by
using his hat to cover
some of the coins. A
parish official is about to
strike the dishonest youth
while his fellow players,
all rascals from the
fringes of London's
underworld, keep their
attention on the game.
Their playing table is the
top of a tomb beside
which lie assorted skulls
and bones dug up during
the excavation of a grave.
Clearly, all these rowdies
have, almost literally, one
foot in the grave.

23

The industrious apprentice is promoted to the countinghouse away from the weavers and spinners. The master rests an arm on his employee's shoulder in a gesture toward one he trusts; indeed, the apprentice even wears a wig, the sign of his newly won gentility, and holds the office keys and daybook of records, tokens of his employer's confidence. The clasped gloves resting on the desk further symbolize his close relationship with the master. In a delightful homely touch, Hogarth shows a potato-faced porter delivering some material while a dog and cat carry on a little spat.

In a scene jammed with dire portents, the idle apprentice is sent to sea by his exasperated master. He has tossed into the ocean his apprenticeship agreement, which begins, "This Indenture . . ." His sea chest reveals his name to be Tho. (short for Thomas) Idle. Tom's mother, seated before him, sheds bitter tears at her son's predicament while two men taunt him. One points toward a gallows on the shore where a corpse hangs; the other dangles a miniature cat-o'-nine-tails to indicate shipboard punishment. Tom, with characteristic irreverence, makes the sign of the horns, the symbol of cuckoldry.

The INDUSTRIOUS 'PRENTICE out of his Time, & Married to his Master's Daughter.

WEST and GOODCHILD

*Proverbs CH:XII. Ver:4.
The Virtuous Woman is a
Crown to her Husband.*

Design'd and Engrav'd by W.m Hogarth.

Plate 6.

Published according to Act of Parliament Sep.t 30. 1.

For the industrious apprentice, life continues to be a series of successes. The morning after his marriage to his master's daughter he leans out the window to pay the head drummer for a serenade, a day-after-the-wedding custom. A male servant spills some of the leavings of the wedding banquet into the apron of a poor woman. A common figure at weddings of the time, Philip in the Tub, a legless beggar who moves about in a wooden bowl, sings a new song, "Jesse, or the Happy Pair." The sign hanging from the building reveals that the apprentice, Francis Goodchild, has been made a partner in the business of his master, Mr. West.

The IDLE 'PRENTICE return'd from Sea, & in a Garret with a common Prostitute.

*Leviticus CHAP:XXVI.Ve 36.
The Sound of a shaken Leaf
shall Chace him.*

Design'd & Engrav'd by W.m Hogarth.

Plate 7

Published according to Act of Parliam.t Sep.t 30.1.

Tom Idle is a nervous wreck. In bed with a prostitute, he is terrified by the sound of a cat chasing a rat down the chimney. He thinks the noise is made by the police, against whom he has barricaded the doors. Tom has grown sick of the sea and taken up highway robbery, as the pistols on the floor indicate. The prostitute, who does not let noises bother her, has Tom's loot spread around her. She displays a morbid interest in an earring in the shape of a gallows, which she holds aloft.

25

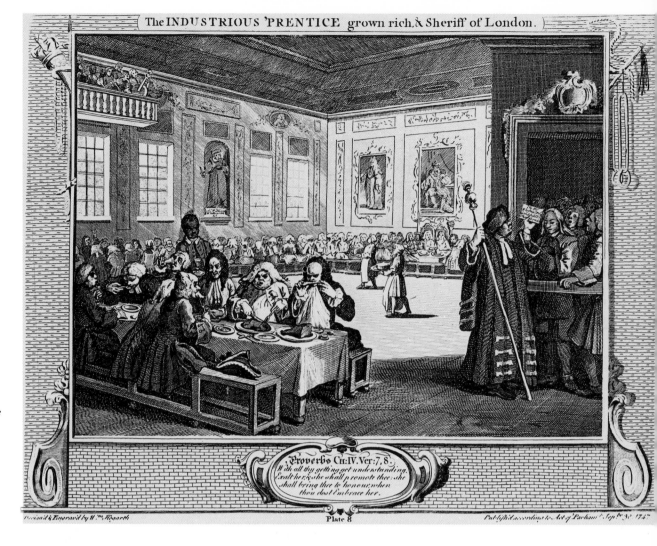

The INDUSTRIOUS 'PRENTICE grown rich,& Sheriff of London.

Goodchild, now a mature man, is honored at a banquet proclaiming him Sheriff of London. He and his wife, as the guests of honor, sit in high-backed chairs under a portrait of King William III (background). A pompous beadle, or usher, carrying a staff, receives a petition for the new sheriff while the assembled guests gorge themselves. Here, as in many of his prints, Hogarth used faces of people well known in London.

Proverbs Ch:IV.Ver:7,8.
With all thy getting get understanding,
Exalt her, & she shall promote thee: she
shall bring thee to honour, when
thou dost Embrace her.

Plate 8

The IDLE 'PRENTICE betray'd by his Whore,& taken in a Night Cellar with his Accomplice.

Even Tom Idle's whore does not remain loyal to him. For a coin, she betrays Tom's whereabouts to the magistrate, who carries his staff of office. The setting is the Blood Bowl House, a London tavern with a highly unsavory reputation. Tom is splitting up the loot with a one-eyed bandit, one of the men he gambled with in the church graveyard (page 23). Meanwhile a man murdered at the inn is being pushed through a trap door as the other patrons of the Blood Bowl brawl and smoke, casually ignoring the crime.

Proverbs CHAP:VI.Ve:26.
The Adulteress will hunt for
the precious life.

Plate 9

Psalm IX. Ver: 16.
The Wicked is snar'd in the
work of his own hands.

Leviticus CH: XIX. Ve: 15.
Thou shalt do no unrighteous
nefs in Judgment.

Plate 10.

Tom Idle is brought before
Francis Goodchild, who
now wears the furred robes
and gold chain of alderman
and acting magistrate. The
one-eyed bandit has turned
on Tom, giving the court
evidence against him. Tom
is sentenced to hang at
London's triple gallows at
Tyburn (below), where
executions sometimes drew
as many as 100,000
spectators. The prisoner,
accompanied by his coffin
and an admonishing
preacher, is carried in a
cart toward the waiting
gallows. A vignette in the
lower right-hand corner
shows two boys, one picking
the pocket of a cake
salesman, while the other
crosses his arms to resist the
temptation to steal the
cakes. Thus the story of
good boy and bad starts
all over again.

The IDLE PRENTICE Executed at Tyburn.

Proverbs CHAP: I. Verf: 27, 28.
When fear cometh as desolation, and their
destruction cometh as a Whirlwind; when
distrefs cometh upon them, then they shall
call upon God, but he will not answer.

Plate II

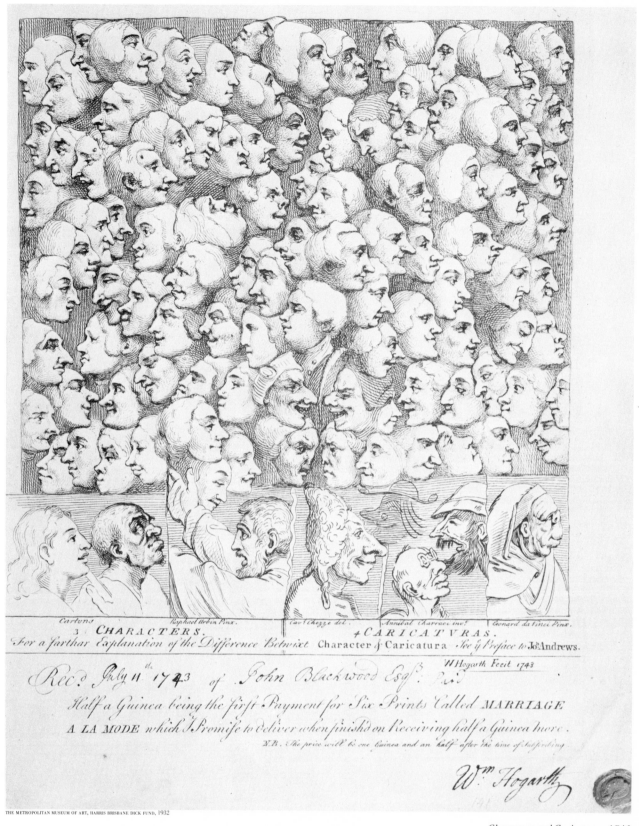

Characters and Caricaturas, 1743

Since Hogarth's work often bordered on exaggeration, it was sometimes dismissed by critics as mere caricature. Hogarth answered these charges in an announcement of his brilliant six-picture-drama *Marriage à la Mode (above).* At the bottom left-hand corner he drew the heads of three Biblical characters based on sketches by Raphael, together with their distortions by other Italian artists. He then filled the remainder of the page with a sea of faces that he claimed represented character rather than caricature.

But *Marriage à la Mode* itself was his best argument. Far from being caricature, it was an astute commentary on the tragedy of arranged marriages, and Hogarth illuminated it with high drama, ironic humor and poignant insights, as the original paintings show.

I

The impoverished Earl of Squanderfield, pointing to his noble family tree, arranges for his son to marry the daughter of a rich city alderman, the piggish-looking man adjusting his glasses. The daughter nervously runs her handkerchief through her engagement ring as the earl's lawyer, Counselor Silvertongue, chats intimately with her. The groom-to-be has eyes only for his own image in a mirror. In the foreground, two dogs chained together provide a broad hint as to the young couple's future.

II

In the early afternoon, not long after their marriage, man and wife are recovering from an evening's pleasures. She is having tea after an all-night card and music party; he sprawls exhausted from a night of dissipation as his dog sniffs another woman's handkerchief drooping from his pocket. Walking away in horror is the newlyweds' steward, who clutches a fistful of bills and only one receipt. Hogarth takes an opportunity here to poke fun at the couple's sterile taste in art, typical of their time. He gibes at their awe of Continental painting and antique statuary, emphasizing the cracked nose of the bust on the mantel.

29

III

The young husband now has a problem—venereal disease. He takes two recent conquests to a quack to see which has infected him. The doctor wipes his glasses in bemused anticipation. The young girl, a servant, weeps in bitter shame. The larger woman, a prostitute, draws a knife to fight rather than submit to examination. The setting of the doctor's office is a triumph of the macabre: the cumbersome machine in the lower right-hand corner is for setting dislocated limbs; a skeleton in the closet makes a suggestive pass at an anatomical model.

IV

The bride, a countess since her father-in-law has died, holds court without her husband. While her hair is being dressed, she chats with Counselor Silvertongue, the lawyer who helped arrange her marriage. Her infatuation with him is obvious: Hogarth has her Negro page pointing at the horns of a figure of the mythological hunter Actaeon; once again the artist has made use of the symbol of a cuckolded husband. The entertainment is provided by a pudgy male singer, accompanied by a flutist.

V

Having inherited the title of Earl of Squanderfield, the young husband rediscovers his honor. He trails his wife to an assignation with Counselor Silvertongue in a private room in a brothel. The cuckolded earl is enraged and a duel ensues in which he is mortally wounded by his wife's lover. The errant wife falls to her knees in shock as her husband dies. Watchmen storm into the room as the counselor, still in night clothes, hastily retreats through the open window.

VI

Hearing that Silvertongue has been hanged at Tyburn for the murder of her husband, the faithless wife commits suicide. She has returned to her father's home, bribed a dim-witted manservant to buy her some poison and swallowed it. An apothecary, called in too late to administer an antidote, berates the servant for buying the poison. An aged maid holds up the dying woman's daughter to kiss her mother goodbye. Since the couple had no son, the title which the wife's father had bought through the marriage contract cannot be perpetuated. The merchant venally removes the ring from his daughter's finger as though to salvage something of value from the marriage à la mode.

Passionate nationalist that he was, Hogarth skewered his country's traditional enemy, France, in his famous painting *O, the Roast Beef of Old England (right)*. The story behind the picture is as engaging as the scene itself. In Calais during his second visit to France in 1748, Hogarth was sketching the gate that the English had built when they occupied the city from 1346 to 1558. Suddenly, a French soldier seized the artist and arrested him as a spy. He was confined to his lodging until the wind was up and he could be shipped home. Hogarth immediately retaliated with this painting.

The scene is a view into Calais from the city's outer gate. The inner gate, the one built by the English and still embossed with the conquerors' arms, looks like a massive face; its portal and drop gate resemble a fanged and gaping mouth, the coat of arms and centerpiece the eyes and forehead. But the picture's main focus is a succulent side of a raw English beef that a cook is delivering to an English eating house. Hogarth is delightedly pointing up the stark difference between life in France and England: his country's celebrated export, the hefty side of beef, appears monumental to the haggard, impoverished residents of Calais. Hogarth, a Protestant, represents the only well-fed person in the scene as a Catholic priest. Two attenuated French soldiers in tricorn hats regard the slab of meat with disbelief; one is so overcome at its enormous size that he spills his bowl of stew. A mercenary Irish soldier sneaks a look while wolfing his stew; another mercenary, a Scot, sits against the wall with his meager repast of barley cake and onion beside him. Slatternly fishwives laugh at the human qualities in the features of a freshly caught skate, unaware that their own expressions are not much different. Hogarth placed himself in the background sketching the gate; the arresting soldier, his pike lowered, has his hand on the artist's shoulder.

O, the Roast Beef of Old England, 1748

Painting of Six Servants' Heads, after 1750

Hogarth dismissed portrait painting as "phizmongering"—peddling faces. Nevertheless he painted one of the finest portraits in English art, *Captain Coram (right).* A sea captain and shipbuilder, Coram made a fortune, but he did not squander it. Instead, he established London's first Foundling Hospital as a haven for the hundreds of babies regularly abandoned on the city's streets. Hogarth, who had no children of his own, supported the Foundling Hospital with his usual gusto. He also used its walls as a showcase of his own works and those of other English painters. (Indirectly, the exhibitions in time led to the creation of London's Royal Academy.) Much as Hogarth railed against the classicized settings that had been used by Continental portraitists like Van Dyck, he himself placed the philanthropic Captain Coram before

a huge marble pillar, with a conventional background of draperies. The remainder of the portrait, however, is all Hogarth: the captain sits in his English scarlet coat, his ships in the distance, the globe at his feet. His solid features, firm mouth, broad brow and compassionate eyes reveal the purposeful, high-minded man whom Hogarth and his contemporaries held in such esteem.

Other Hogarth portraits reflect this same preoccupation with middle-class virtues. As a result his sitters all seem to bear the same stamp. But the studies he made of his servants *(above)* escape this fault. These gentle portraits are deeply felt remembrances of people the artist loved. Placed at random on the canvas, they show the clarity and honesty that reflect the sympathetic view of human nature that underlies all of Hogarth's work.

Captain Coram, 1740

CHARTER
HOUSE.
Gainsborough 1748.

II

The Country Painter

Trying to make a name for himself in London, Gainsborough followed an example set by Hogarth and donated this painting to the city's Foundling Hospital, where artists had found an unusual but effective showcase. Gainsborough probably hoped, as other aspiring painters did, that charity-working aristocrats would notice his picture and commission an original from him. One of a series of townscapes, the painting shows another London institution, Sutton's Hospital, also known as The Charterhouse.

The Charterhouse (Sutton's Hospital), 1748

During Gainsborough's early years in London he kept close ties with Sudbury, returning to his birthplace periodically to visit his family's home. On one of these visits he met Margaret Burr, the girl who was to become his wife. There is a good deal of mystery about her origin. She is variously described by Gainsborough's biographers as "a Scots girl of low birth" and as the sister of a salesman in John Gainsborough's cloth business. But a high-ranking nobleman, the Duke of Beaufort, took a more than casually beneficent interest in her future, and in later life she herself hinted that there was royal blood in her veins. Everybody agrees that she was exceedingly pretty, and Allan Cunningham, an early biographer, tells how the couple met: "It happened in one of Gainsborough's pictorial excursions among the woods of Suffolk, that he sat down to make a sketch of some fine trees, with sheep reposing below and wood-doves roosting above, when a young woman entered unexpectedly upon the scene, and was at once admitted into the landscape and the feelings of the artist." A later biographer, George Williams Fulcher, describes how the meeting led to marriage: "The memory of Miss Burr's extraordinary beauty is still preserved in Sudbury; and that a beautiful girl should wish to have her portrait painted by her brother's young friend, naturally followed as cause and effect. The sittings were numerous and protracted, but the likeness was at last finished, and pronounced by competent judges, perfect. The young lady expressed her warm admiration of the Painter's skill, and in doing so, gave him the gentlest possible hint that perhaps in time he might become the possessor of the original. On that hint he spake, and, after a short courtship, was rewarded by her hand and with it an annuity of two hundred pounds."

Two hundred pounds! In Gainsborough's day £200 a year was a comfortable income indeed. A skilled artisan considered himself lucky if he earned £50 a year, and a clerk in a sought-after government position seldom got more. Gainsborough was anything but mercenary, and Margaret Burr was so attractive that he could not be called a fortune hunter for wanting to marry her. Nevertheless her annuity was to have an important influence on his career. It is also another piece of evidence in the

The play of light and shadow in this etching reflects young Gainsborough's admiration for the work of the 17th Century Dutch landscapist Jacob van Ruisdael. Ruisdael felt that the most profound aspect of nature was its continual movement. In Gainsborough's design, sunlight filters through the trees and briefly dapples the cows as they move across the forest floor; but soon, one feels, the sun will slip behind a cloud sailing across the sky.

mystery of Margaret's origin, as are the circumstances that surrounded her wedding.

Tom and his pretty bride were married in 1746, when he was 19 and she a year younger. But the ceremony did not take place in Sudbury, but rather in the London "marrying chapel" operated by a Dr. Keith. This has been taken to indicate that it was a runaway marriage against the wishes of Tom's parents, and there is foundation for this belief in the suggestion by some authorities that Margaret Burr was illegitimate, a serious matter in the respectable middle-class society to which Gainsborough belonged. There is evidence pointing to the Duke of Beaufort as her father, which would bear out her claim to noble blood. If this is true, her mother could have been either a duke's decorative mistress or a servant girl gotten with child by a young lord, as frequently happened in aristocratic houses. In any case it was the Duke of Beaufort who settled on her the generous annuity of £200, which was faithfully paid all her life through the bank of the Messrs. Hoare in London, which kept its clients' secrets.

Because of his wife's annuity, Gainsborough was never forced during his early manhood to come to terms with the bleak necessity of earning a living by painting. He was never a slave to sitters for portraits. He felt free to make frequent excursions into the countryside, sketching interesting scenes and soaking up memories of light and shadow, trees, brooks, clouds, farm people and their cottages, wandering gypsies, cattle, dogs and horses. He could put together landscapes out of what he had seen and not care very much if no one bought them. He could paint delightful portraits of his children, his friends and his friends' pretty wives. He could sell them for next to nothing or give them away, and when a paying sitter demanded that his portrait be painted in a rigidly conventional manner, he might or might not comply.

During his youth and young manhood Gainsborough's self-sufficiency permitted him to experiment and follow his instincts and fancies. Even when he had won commercial success in a larger world, he never lost his habit of independence. Though he became enormously successful as a fashionable portrait painter—honored, much in demand and very well paid —his style remained individual. To the very end of his life it was changeable, experimental, young and gay.

While Gainsborough achieved fame during his lifetime, the voluminous chitchat written in 18th Century England seldom mentions him. This was mostly his own fault. He did not like or cultivate literary men or women, as many of his colleagues did. His good friends, of which he had many, were not the sort who produce diaries or memoirs, so detailed information about his life is comparatively meager. Luckily he was an excellent and colorful correspondent, and a number of his letters have been saved.

Few biographies have been written about him, and those are dull, clumsy and contradictory. The authors who wrote shortly after his death made little or no effort to interview Gainsborough's friends, while later writers, influenced by the nice-nellyism of the Victorian period, passed over with righteous forbearance those things about him that they considered unseemly. Even some of his letters to friends suffered from Victorian cover-up. "Licencious language" was removed by later owners, who tore out pieces of the letters so they could be shown without provoking blushes.

Enough information survives, however, to prove that Gainsborough was an attractive and interesting man, and his paintings themselves are unusually autobiographical. More than most painters, he talked with his brush and left in his pictures an eloquent record of himself. In his earliest known painting, done when he was 18, this autobiographical quality is already apparent. The picture is of a miscellaneous dog named Bumper, described on the back of the canvas as "a most remarkable sagacious Cur." Art critics with the advantage of hindsight see in the background of this unpretentious work some hint of the way Gainsborough would later paint his landscapes. But the picture also reveals the warm nature of the artist himself and clearly shows his characteristic fondness for humble, ordinary animals. Though Bumper certainly boasts no pedigree, he looks intelligent, playful, humorous and affectionate, just the sort of dog most boys would love.

Following his marriage in London in 1746, Tom and his bride seem to have remained in the city for a few years, but where they lived or what friends they had is not known. During this time Gainsborough painted portraits and landscapes, some of which he sold for small sums. Most of these have disappeared; only a few are left to prove that he was now painting seriously and had reached some degree of acceptance. Among the survivors is a small round picture, only 22 inches in diameter, called *The Charterhouse (page 36)*, which he gave to London's Foundling Hospital in 1748. Because the city lacked a public gallery, such a donation to a well-known institution was one of the few ways that a young artist could exhibit his work. The picture is painted with academic precision, but the children playing in a patch of sunlight and the group of trees posed like ballet dancers give it unusual life and gaiety.

Gainsborough's personal possessions were elegantly simple. Shown above are the ornamented brass tamper *(left)* with which he packed his pipe, and his snuffbox. Snuffboxes of the period were often made of precious material carved in exotic designs, but Gainsborough's was a relatively plain wooden box with ivory and silver inlay, engraved with his initials. Below is the artist's mahogany work cabinet; its lid lifts up to form an easel and the drawers are partitioned to hold supplies of dry pigments.

In that same year Gainsborough's father died, and Tom and his wife returned to Sudbury, perhaps to help settle the family estate. How long they stayed there is not certain, but it was long enough for them to become the parents of two daughters, their only children. It was probably in Sudbury that he finished (or more likely wholly repainted) a landscape that he had started in his schoolboy years. It is variously called *Gainsborough's Forest* or *Cornard Wood (pages 54-55)*. It earned him no recorded acclaim at the time, but today it hangs proudly in London's National Gallery and is considered one of his finest works.

Cornard Wood does not represent any particular place. The objects and persons that form the composition came from Gainsborough's sketches or his remarkable visual memory. It is interesting to observe how he assembled them. The main theme is a narrow dirt road winding through a wood near a slow-flowing brook. A man on horseback and a countryman trudging along the road with a pack on his back and a dog at his heels give a sense of movement and direction. Other actors in the roadside drama include a pair of donkeys; one of them with ears pricked forward is watching the artist. A woodcutter is tying up a bundle of branches while his dog sleeps close by. Near the road is a young man digging clay or gravel, and a pretty girl has come along to keep him company. All these points of living interest lead the eye along the road and at last through a gap in the trees to a distant patch of sunlit fields and the roofs of an even more distant village.

The people and animals are important in Gainsborough's plan, but even more important are the trees, which dominate the scene. They are old, gnarled trees, parts of a dense wild forest where man is an intruder, but they are marshaled in a way that shows them to be on the edge of the forest. Man's domain, the cultivated land, lies just beyond.

Every detail in *Cornard Wood* is painted with meticulous care, showing the influence of the naturalistic Dutch landscape painters Gainsborough admired. The leaves of the nearer trees are shown individually. Blades of grass, clumps of weeds and the lichen on the tree trunks are minutely delineated as if they were meant to be looked at from about 10 inches away.

This painstaking realism is not slavish copying of nature, for Gainsborough never let realism interfere with his composition. In *Cornard Wood,* for instance, the level of the water in the brook is several feet above that of the road. Unless a dam is hidden behind a tree, which is most unlikely, the water would naturally run downhill and make the road a stream bed. Gainsborough must have realized this, but for the sake of his composition he wanted the water at a certain height, and he did not care at all if it was unrealistic.

Some time after finishing *Cornard Wood,* Gainsborough and his wife left Sudbury and moved to Ipswich, a larger town about 15 miles away and at the head of the Orwell estuary, where he would have a better chance of making a living as a portrait painter. They rented a small house on Lower Brook Street, which is now in an industrial district near the waterfront. The house must have been very small indeed, for its rent was only six pounds per year.

Ipswich, one of the principal towns of Suffolk, then had about 10,000 people, many of them concerned with the wool business. The Industrial Revolution had not begun, and Suffolk's ancient trade of hand weaving had not yet been ruined by the competition of machine-made cloth from the north of England, which had water power and coal for running steam engines. The town was old, with narrow, crooked streets and many blocks of medieval houses. It was certainly provincial, but like other provincial centers in a predominantly agricultural England it was also something of a cultural hub that attracted the landowners from the surrounding area. Country squires, gentlemen grown prosperous because of protective tariffs on agricultural products, lived in beautiful manor houses, most of which still stand today, and were masters of swarms of servants and semifeudal retainers. For entertainment beyond hunting and shooting they put on their powdered wigs, dressed their women in all the glory of 18th Century finery and went to provincial centers such as Ipswich, which had fine shops, concerts, dances and merry inns. To these lively towns came even the greatest titled landowners, some of whom dominated whole counties and who preferred to spend most of the year on their country estates, visiting London only for sessions of Parliament or for a brief social season. Ipswich was not bustling, boisterous London, of course, but when Gainsborough moved there he certainly did not feel that he was submerging himself in dullness. He could look forward to good times.

For a while paying customers for portraits were few, and Tom filled out his time with his beloved sketching and with any painting job he could find. There is some evidence that he did coach, sign and house painting. Such work was not as lowly as it sounds. Shopkeepers' signs and the panels of gentlemen's coaches were commonly bright with elaborate scenes whose painting called for considerable skill if not for creativeness. Houses were not usually painted on the outside. They were constructed of brick, stone or stucco that needed no paint, and house painting meant decorating the interior walls and ceilings with pictures and other ornamentation. Often the work paid well, probably as well as the lower grades of portrait painting.

During this early period in Ipswich there is no record that Tom sold any of his landscapes, which were what he most wanted to paint, but sitters for portraits began to appear. At first he painted them mostly in couples and in miniature full length, a modification of the conversation piece that he had learned from the dissolute Hayman in London, and he managed to smuggle a good deal of landscape into several of them. One of these portrait-plus-landscape pictures, that of Mr. and Mrs. Robert Andrews, was probably painted not later than 1750 and is generally agreed to be one of his early masterpieces.

Robert Andrews was a young country squire with lands in the neighborhood of Ipswich. Gainsborough shows him leaning against a decorative bench beneath a noble tree, in rather dressy hunting costume and a three-cornered hat and carrying a shotgun under his arm. His dog stands at his feet, looking up admiringly. Mrs. Andrews sits on the bench, the full skirt of her blue silk dress covering nearly all of it. Behind them is a rolling landscape; the strong-limbed trees standing around like people, the distant sheep, the sheaves of reaped grain and the glimpse of a house through a copse are carefully arranged to give a feeling of spaciousness. The view is of typical Suffolk farm country which, with minor additions such as tractors, looks much the same today.

The clouds, as always in Gainsborough's pictures, are an important part of the composition, their gradation from dark to light adding brilliance to the sunlit fields. They are very English clouds. In the United States a dark gray cloud such as the one in the left-hand background would mean heavy rain, perhaps a thunderstorm, but in England dark clouds are common and usually inoffensive. They drift across country continually, dropping only light sprinkles of rain, and are mingled with blue sky to create what English weather forecasters call "intervals of sunlight." Nothing makes a landscape look more English than proper English clouds.

Mr. and Mrs. Andrews are both looking directly at the artist, as Gainsborough's sitters often did. This is the most demanding attitude for the portraitist; it almost compels him to look in their eyes and tell with his brush what kind of people they are and what they are thinking. In the case of the Andrews couple, Gainsborough does just this with startling success. Young Squire Andrews is a bit weak and soft, and his lips are rather too full for a man. Perhaps he wanted to be shown with his gun and dog just because he was unsure of himself. He looks suspicious, almost hostile, as if resenting the close inspection that the handsome young painter is, of necessity, giving his pretty wife.

Mrs. Andrews is a stronger character. Her lips are firmly set, but she knows she is attractive and intends to make the most of it while remaining in command of all situations. She is looking at the painter with almost shameless appraisal, as if she were speculating during the hours of posing what kind of lover he would make. Gainsborough made the young Andrews couple live forever, but in doing so he cast some doubt on whether their marriage would be happy.

Gainsborough did not always paint his sitters with such revealing characterization. Sometimes he merely copied their faces with near-photographic accuracy and let it go at that. Perhaps the sitter did not interest him, or perhaps he saw something in his face that he did not like and so preferred to give the portrait a neutral character rather than an unpleasantly revealing one. Only such personal reactions to the sitters can explain the unevenness of his early portraits. Some are stiff and dull; others are wonderfully lively and full of character.

Landscapes painted in Ipswich show that Gainsborough was influenced but by no means carried away by foreign artistic fashions. His charming *Woodcutter Courting a Milkmaid,* for instance, proves that he had admired archly bucolic pictures by French contemporaries such as Boucher. The pretty milkmaid wears a provocative low-necked dress reminiscent of those favored by the French painters but one which no English peasant mother would have permitted her daughter to wear to work. Both she and the handsome young woodcutter (who has cut very little wood) are stock figures from French pastoral fantasies, but the rest of the picture is pure Gainsborough.

The most prominent character in the scene, much more conspicuous than the boy and girl, is the gnarled, hollow trunk of an almost dead oak, resembling any one of a number sketched by Gainsborough during his tramps in the country. He lovingly shows every bump and knothole, every place where the wood has tried to grow over the stub of a broken-off limb. He loved dying trees whose exposed limbs and barkless trunks made dramatic patterns for him to play with. Even now Suffolk has plenty of them. They stand stubbornly in pastures, their bare limbs gesticulating out of tufts of foliage. Many of these modern "Gainsborough trees" would fit nicely into Gainsborough landscapes.

Woodcutter Courting a Milkmaid has other characteristic Gainsborough touches. The weeds near the tree (Gainsborough admired weeds) are painted with sufficient accuracy to show their species. They are burdock and Queen Anne's lace. The horses at the left are tired farm horses returning from a hard day's work (Gainsborough loved farm horses), and the man who follows them is tired too. The horses are not, however, pulling a plow, as city-bred critics have assumed. The implement has two wheels and the axle between them carries some sort of container. It looks like a grain drill, a device for planting grain in furrows instead of sowing it broadcast. Tom Gainsborough had reason to be familiar with grain drills; his older brother, the Reverend Humphry Gainsborough, invented one, and very likely this is it.

While entertaining himself and his viewers with many carefully chosen and painted details, Gainsborough was always concerned with the overall effect. In *Woodcutter Courting a Milkmaid* he evoked the marvelous peace that comes at the end of a rural working day. The sun is low in the sky, as the shadows on the tree trunk plainly show. The milkmaid's pail is full; she and her handsome woodcutter friend (who looks a little like Gainsborough's self-portraits) will now have a bit of agreeable flirtation before going home. The horses and their driver are headed for the village, a typical Suffolk village whose church has a square tower without a steeple, as most Suffolk churches do today. Everything in the picture speaks of the pleasant moment when the day's work is done. Only countrymen know the sensuous pleasure of this moment.

During his seven or eight years in Ipswich, Gainsborough led a carefree and apparently unambitious life. In spite of the small size of the town, he was not a prominent citizen. Not a word about him appeared in the news columns of Ipswich newspapers published during his stay. He did no self-advertising, joined no societies that might make him better known and help his portrait business. This obscurity is not surprising, since in mid-18th Century England the profession of artist conferred little status. On occasion Gainsborough may have dressed with some elegance, and he is known to have worn a wig, which was a symbol of some social standing. His friends in Ipswich were mostly middle-class people on the same level as his burgher relatives in Sudbury—merchants, small manufacturers, physicians, minor clergymen and local officials. They might be educated, but they were hardly aristocratic. The true aristocrats lived on their country estates, and if Gainsborough ever went to one of their manor houses to paint portraits (there is little evidence that he did at this time), his genial personality probably would have won him a pleasant reception, but he would not have been accepted as an equal. Any meals that he might have eaten there would have been taken with the more important servants.

Gainsborough's chief recreation in Ipswich, aside from painting —which was not exactly work—was music. He played the violin fairly well, and many of his best friends were either amateur or professional musicians. He belonged to an informal music club whose meetings were sometimes very merry indeed, with more drinking than music making. Long after, in 1797, the landscape painter John Constable, who had sought recollections of Gainsborough among Ipswich ancients, reported: "He was generally the butt of the company, and his wig was to them a fund of amusement, as it was often snatched from his head and thrown about the room."

A few other memories of Gainsborough survived in and around Ipswich. The son of a clergyman in nearby Southwold, writing to a friend, said: "I remember Gainsborough well, he was a great favorite of my father; indeed his affable and agreeable manners endeared him to all with whom his profession brought him in contact, either at the cottage or the castle; there was that peculiar bearing which could not fail to leave a pleasing impression. Many houses in Suffolk, as well as in the neighboring county, were always open to him, and their owners thought it an honor to entertain him. I have seen the aged features of the peasantry lit up with a grateful recollection of his many acts of kindness and benevolence. My father's residence bears testimony alike to his skill as a painter and his kindness as a man, for the panels of several of the rooms are adorned with the productions of his genius. In one, is a picture of Gainsborough's two daughters, when young [*page 50*]; they were engaged in chasing a butterfly; the arrangement of the figures, and the landscape introduced into the background, are of the most charming description."

This now-priceless picture, one of the most delightful portraits of children ever painted, hangs today in the National Gallery, London. It was apparently a gift to the Southwold clergyman. Other early triumphs of Gainsborough's poetic imagination were also given away to friends, and to the end of his life he remained just as generous.

Like most portrait painters whose paying sitters are too few to keep them busy, Gainsborough painted his family—especially his daughters —over and over again. Always he portrayed the children as delicate, sensitive, vulnerable, as if the world were too harsh a place for them to be happy in. He also painted himself, not flatteringly but as a gently handsome young man with sympathetic eyes. Twice at least he painted himself with his wife. She is certainly pretty, but she does not have the wonderful charm that he gave to many other women. A portrait of her not many years after their marriage shows that she had grown quite stout. Gainsborough's friends agreed that she also became excessively penurious, opposing every expenditure by her husband.

As soon as Gainsborough was earning money on his own to augment his wife's annuity, he left his six-pounds-a-year house and moved to a much more comfortable house opposite the municipal and county building known as the Shire Hall. It was in a better part of Ipswich, where he could enjoy the trees and flowers of neighboring gardens. Some of his friends now were the kind of person that a young painter should know. One of these was William Wollaston, a fellow music lover who represented Ipswich in Parliament. Tom painted his portrait twice, once holding a flute, and made him look like a very amiable rascal, nice to have around at any time and especially when a bit of influence is needed. A very different sort of friend was Joshua Kirby, a house and coach painter who was also a picture dealer. Kirby was a religious man—so religious that he was the only lay member of the local clergymen's club —but Gainsborough, who was not religiously inclined, was deeply attached to him. He painted him several times. The portraits clearly show the affection with which he always illuminated the faces of friends whom he really loved.

Another close friend was Samuel Kilderbee, the Ipswich town clerk. Tom painted his picture at least twice and showed him as pleasant but not particularly interesting. Kilderbee's wife was another matter. She was not really beautiful, but Gainsborough painted her in a low-necked dress and high-swept hair, with a curl of it coiled lovingly against her neck, and made her something wonderful. She is looking straight at the artist, and her eyes are as warmly inviting as her full lips. It takes no knowledge of painting to see that she was an extraordinarily sensual woman. Her portrait is now in the Ipswich museum where one of the uniformed guards, pointing it out to a visitor recently, remarked, "We have her husband here too. I don't know how he handled her."

Some time after Gainsborough had moved to his new home opposite the Shire Hall, a man came into his life who was to become his first important patron and who would change the direction and pace of his career. In 1753 Philip Thicknesse was appointed Lieutenant Governor of Landguard Fort at Harwich, 12 miles down the Orwell River from Ipswich. Governor Thicknesse was related to several titled families and was

This English guitar belonged to Gainsborough, an enthusiastic amateur musician. The instrument, an evolved form of lute called a cittern, was imported from the Continent into Britain around the middle of the 18th Century and became extremely popular. How well Gainsborough played it is uncertain—after his death his biographers engaged in some public squabbling about whether he could even read music—but everyone agreed on his zeal. He drew the pleasant little sketch at left to commemorate what he found a most enjoyable pastime: making music with agreeable companions. Among his convivial fellow players on similar occasions was Johann Christian Bach, the youngest son of the great composer.

well acquainted in aristocratic society. As a youth he had emigrated to the American colony of Georgia and later captained an independent company of soldiers in Jamaica. He was, however, a contentious person, and it is surprising that he and the easygoing Gainsborough could ever become friendly. One of the artist's early biographers describes the Governor as a man who was "perpetually imagining insult, and would sniff an injury from afar." During his governorship of Landguard Fort a quarrel with another officer led to a court-martial on libel charges and Thicknesse was convicted and imprisoned for three months. In later years he fell into serious financial straits when the court refused to grant him an expected inheritance, and for a while he seems to have supported himself by blackmailing his enemies. But despite his unpleasant and argumentative ways, he always remained a devoted friend of Gainsborough's.

Just after the artist's death, Thicknesse wrote a short biography of him in one day. It is hasty, prejudiced in some ways and contains errors, but it is a work of real affection and provides the best firsthand information about Gainsborough's lovable and interesting character.

"To do Mr. Gainsborough justice," Thicknesse wrote toward the beginning of his book, "it requires a pen equal to his own inimitable pencil, to hold forth the powers it possessed, or the tender feelings of his heart, a task I am by no means adequate to, but as I can with truth boast that I was the first man who perceived, though through clouds of bad coloring, what an accurate eye he possessed, and the truth of his drawing, and who dragged him from the obscurity of a Country Town at a time that all his neighbors were as ignorant of his great talents as he was himself."

Thicknesse' account tells of the amusing circumstances that led him to meet the artist: "While I was walking with the then printer and editor of the Ipswich Journal, in a very pretty town garden of his, I perceived a melancholy-faced countryman, with his arms locked together, leaning over the garden wall. I pointed him out to the printer, who was a very ingenious man, and he with great gravity of face, said the man had been there all day, and that he pitied him, believing he was either mad or miserable. I then stepped forward with an intention to speak to the *madman,* and did not perceive, until I was close up, that it was a *wooden man* painted up on a shaped board. Mr. Creighton (I think that was the printer's name) told me I had not been the only person this inimitable deception had imposed upon, for that many of his acquaintance had been led even to speak to it, before they perceived it to be a work of art; and upon finding the artist himself lived in that town, I immediately procured his address, visited Mr. Gainsborough, and I told him I came to chide him for having imposed a shadow instead of a substance upon me." This cutout board is now in Christchurch Mansion Museum at Ipswich. Its paint is too dark with age to fool anyone today, but it is pleasant evidence of Gainsborough's light-hearted temperament.

Thicknesse continues: "Mr. Gainsborough received me in his painting room, in which stood several portraits, truely drawn, perfectly like, but stiffly painted, and worse colored . . . but when I turned my eyes to his little landscapes and drawings, I was charmed, these were the works of fancy and gave him infinite delight. MADAM NATURE, NOT MAN, was then

This painted wooden cutout led to the meeting between Gainsborough and his first important patron, Philip Thicknesse. To show his skill at portraiture and to play a little joke, Gainsborough had made the 15-inch-high figure—using the likeness of a man he had one day surprised enviously eying the pears in his garden—and set it up on a wall to fool passersby. Thicknesse saw it, was deceived and amused, and sought out the artist. Later, Thicknesse not only bought pictures from Gainsborough but advised him and promoted his career.

his only study, and he seemed intimately acquainted with that BEAUTIFUL OLD LADY.

"Soon after this, the late King passed by the garrisons under my command, and as I wanted a subject to employ Mr. Gainsborough's pencil in the landscape way, I desired him to come and eat a dinner with me, and take down in his pocket book the particulars of the Fort, the adjacent hills, and the distant view of Harwich, in order to form a landscape of the Yachts passing the garrison under the salute of the guns, of the size of a panel over my chimney piece, he accordingly came and in a short time after brought the picture. I was much pleased with the performance, and asking him the price? he modestly said, he hoped I would not think fifteen guineas too much. I assured him that in my opinion it would (if offered to be sold in London) produce double that sum, and accordingly I paid him, thanked him and lent him an excellent fiddle."

Thicknesse took the picture of Landguard Fort to London and had an engraving made of it. The picture itself was ruined by leaning against a wet wall, but Thicknesse reported with his usual freedom from modesty: "That engraving made Mr. Gainsborough's name known beyond the circle of his country residence, and he was soon after by me, and several of his friends, urged to remove to Bath, and try his talents at portrait painting in that fluctuating city, at which time I had a house there and resided during the winters."

Thicknesse and his friends were not the only persons who urged Gainsborough to move to the ultrafashionable resort city of Bath in southwestern England. The artist's oldest sister, Mary Gibbon, had already moved there with her husband and kept a lodginghouse. The painter from provincial Ipswich would not be alone in what must have been a rather daunting place.

Shortly after he met Gainsborough, Lieutenant Governor Philip Thicknesse commissioned the artist to paint a "chimney piece," a picture meant to hang over a fireplace mantel. The subject Thicknesse chose was Landguard Fort, the coastal garrison he governed—shown below in an engraving made from the painting. The fort itself was an unattractive structure, so Gainsborough de-emphasized it by placing it in the background, enlivening the foreground with rustic figures and animals.

The People of Home

When Gainsborough returned from a London apprenticeship to his native Suffolk he was still in his early twenties, but he had learned a good deal about how to succeed in the art trade. Although he preferred landscape painting, he had discovered, as he later wrote a friend, that "in mine [profession] a Man may do great things and starve in a Garret if he does not . . . conform . . . in chusing the branch [of painting] which they will encourage & pay for." Thus, he set out to perfect his skills at portraiture, in those days the principal and most lucrative source of commissions. At first his style was stiff and awkward, not unlike that of dozens of other provincial artists. But soon his brush became freer and more adept; his knack for catching a likeness and evoking a meaningful expression became instinctive. Using his family *(right),* the most available models, he worked to perfect his technique, often leaving canvases unfinished after he got the gesture or fall of fabric he was after.

Gainsborough never stopped thinking about landscape, however, and he continued to paint Suffolk in all its rich greenery. He also began to integrate complete and convincing landscapes into the backgrounds of some of his portraits, giving the sitters a bonus that they probably neither expected nor paid for. These works were never duplicated; they stand as landmarks in the career of a man who found a way to succeed at his craft without sacrificing either principle or pleasure.

Gainsborough's group portrait of himself, his wife and their first child, Margaret, reveals his major interests at the time he painted it: the rich fabrics, the billowing gown, the elegant but informal pose, all reflect the influence of French painters whose work he had admired in London. In the lacy foliage and hazy mass of trees, he reveals his own developing style of treating landscape.

Thomas Gainsborough, His Wife and Daughter, c. 1751-1752

49

The Painter's Daughters Chasing a Butterfly, late 1750s

R ejoicing in a gift just realized," as one critic put it, the young Gainsborough created in these portraits of his daughters two of the loveliest paintings of children in all art. He was seldom able to hide his true feelings when he painted and he gave his gifts most fully when he portrayed people he loved; nowhere do they seem greater than in these portraits of Mary, the younger, and Margaret.

Above, the girls chase a butterfly, their hands as well as their tender faces reflecting Gainsborough's growing ability to express grace. At right they are shown a few years older in a sweet, sisterly embrace. Neither of these pictures was for sale, and Gainsborough did not bother to finish them. He barely blocked in the details of dress and background foliage in the full-length portrait; in the other

The Painter's Daughters Teasing a Cat, late 1750s

he lightly sketched a playful pet cat in Margaret's arms and then apparently changed his mind about including the animal.

If Gainsborough's children are revealed as solemn, unsmiling youngsters, there is good reason. The daughters, whom the painter whimsically called Molly and the Captain, were troubled girls who grew to be unstable women. Margaret often behaved erratically. She was an excellent harpsichordist, and after her father became famous, word of her talent reached Queen Charlotte, who expressed an interest in hearing her play. For no apparent reason Margaret flew into a temper at the royal request and refused. Mary married a musician friend of her father's, but they parted, and she later went insane.

Mr. and Mrs. Andrews, c. 1748

Gainsborough's early experiments combining landscape and portraiture led to delightful paintings of Suffolk and its gentry. His portrait of John Plampin *(above, right),* is especially interesting because he copied his basic idea for the figure's pose almost exactly from the French rococo painter Antoine Watteau, who had depicted an elegantly dressed aristocrat reclining in a leafy bower and gesturing toward four naked nymphs and a satyr. Gainsborough was unusually inventive and seldom borrowed from other painters, even old masters, although the practice was common among his fellows. But here he duplicated the position of the legs, the left hand, the angle of the head and even the attitude of the dog. In his variation, however, a panorama of English parkland replaces the scene of pastoral revelry and Squire Plampin tucks his right hand, rather self-consciously, into his waistcoat. Gainsborough may have been inspired to make use of the Watteau work because Plampin looked uncannily like the man in the French picture: the chance to play a little art-historical joke may have proved

John Plampin, early 1750s

irresistible to the young painter.

Little is owed to France and a great deal to Gainsborough's pleasure in the Suffolk landscape in the painting he made of Mr. and Mrs. Robert Andrews *(above, left)*. Indeed, the picture is as much a portrait of the Andrews' rolling farmland at Auberies as it is of the young couple. But the artist has caught his sitters perfectly: the bland-faced new husband tries to look as nonchalant as an experienced lord of the manor; his pretty wife sits with a firm and steady gaze suggesting a forceful

character behind her girlish façade.

Although most Gainsborough paintings have been sold and resold many times, the Andrews double portrait has had an unusually stable and appropriately rural existence. It remained at Auberies in the Andrews family estate from around 1750, when it was painted, until 1961, when the young squire's great-great-great-grandson finally offered it for sale at auction. Along with the Plampin, the painting is now one of the chief treasures of 18th Century portraiture in London's National Gallery.

Greatest among Gainsborough's early landscapes is *Cornard Wood,* a picture so identified with the artist that it is often called *Gainsborough's Forest.* Probably begun during his Sudbury school days, when he was about 13, and finished or repainted in 1748, when he was 21 and had just returned to Suffolk from London, the scene summarizes all his youthful preoccupations and developing abilities. The most evident qualities are his skill at conveying the atmosphere of hot summer tranquillity and the precise depiction of a profusion of natural details: leaves, twigs, grasses, clouds. Like the modest Dutch landscapes that were popular in Suffolk homes during Gainsborough's boyhood, *Cornard Wood* is a loving celebration of a specific place at a moment in time.

A French influence can also be seen in the casual disposition of the figures in the landscape and in the soft modeling of their features and garments. Yet the painting appears reportorial. Even today a tourist in Suffolk could expect to come upon such a view—a turning road, farmers at simple tasks, a tiny church tower glinting in the distance. The naturalness of the scene is contrived, however, for Gainsborough assembled this tiny corner of England from many observations in various parts of Suffolk and over a long time. Distilled in his imagination, the picture lives. He would paint others with more originality and a freer brush, but few with more charm.

Cornard Wood (Gainsborough's Forest), c. 1748

III

Fame in Fashionable Bath

When Gainsborough moved from Ipswich to Bath in 1759, he entered another world. Ipswich was quiet, provincial, with not many rich or aristocratic inhabitants, while Bath was England's most fashionable winter resort, crammed with wealth and rank. It shone with silk and glittered with jewels, and the gilded coaches of dukes and earls were common and spectacular sights on its streets. Gainsborough's worldly friend, Governor Thicknesse, was right in his recommendation; Bath was the ideal place for an unknown but gifted portrait painter to win fame and fortune.

For a winter resort the site of Bath was anything but favorable. The old city crowded uncomfortably into the narrow, steep-sided valley of the River Avon, and its climate was damp and chilly. But it had an important asset: a group of hot springs—a great rarity in England—that yielded half a million gallons per day of mildly saline and reputedly healing water at 120° F., about as hot as can be bathed in with equanimity.

In Gainsborough's time the people of Bath firmly believed that their city was founded by Bladud, a king of the ancient Britons and father of the King Lear immortalized by Shakespeare. When Bladud was a young prince, so the story goes, he caught leprosy, and his father, King Hudibras, regretfully sent him into exile to keep his disease from infecting the court. For a long time he wandered and at last came to the village of Keynsham on the Avon, where he got a job tending hogs. All went well until the hogs caught leprosy from him. To keep their owner from noticing what had happened, the Prince herded the hogs across the river into uninhabited territory in search, he said, of better acorns.

After rooting through the woods for a while, the hogs found a pool of steaming water, stampeded into it and wallowed in the mud. When they came out they were cured of leprosy. Prince Bladud followed their example, bathed in the miraculous water, and was cured too. Back he went to his father's court and was greeted with rejoicing. When in due course he became king, he founded Bath beside the health-giving hot springs and made it a glorious capital from which he ruled for many years. In his old age he got the idea that he could fly, lashed artificial wings on his arms and was killed when he jumped off the roof of a temple.

While he was establishing his reputation as a first-class portraitist at Bath, Gainsborough painted his best-known work, *The Blue Boy*, the most popular picture in English art. The identity of the model, however, was long surrounded by mystery: no one knows for certain who the sitter was or when and why Gainsborough painted him. He is now believed to have been Jonathan Buttall, the teen-age son of a rich London hardware dealer. Painter and subject evidently became fast friends, for Buttall was one of the small group of people Gainsborough wished to attend his funeral.

The Blue Boy, 1770

In medieval times this engaging tale was actively promoted by Bath's equivalent of a modern Chamber of Commerce to emphasize the healing power of the town's hot mineral water, but there is little or no fact behind it. The Britons may have made some use of the hot springs, but they built no city there. The first to exploit the site were the Roman conquerors of Britain, who had a favorite custom of bathing in mineral water to cure almost any ailment, or merely for pleasure. In the First Century A.D. they discovered the hot springs and built around them a small but elegant Roman-style town that they named Aquae Sulis (Waters of Sul) after a local deity. For the next three centuries Aquae Sulis was probably the pleasantest place in what the Romans must have considered a cold and dreary province of their empire. Battle-weary soldiers and rheumatic officials came there to bask in the hot water, which flowed through lead pipes into large baths like shallow swimming pools. Some of the carved stonework of these Roman structures still survives and so do the remains of sudatoria (sweat rooms) heated by clay flues under the floor.

After the Romans evacuated Britain, Aquae Sulis fell into decay; the buildings tumbled down and were covered with river silt, but the hot springs still flowed. When the invading Anglo-Saxons found them in the Fifth Century, they renamed the place Hatum Bathum, from which the modern name descends. During the Middle Ages, as tales of wondrous cures emanated from Bath, the town slowly regained its fame as a health resort, and by the 16th Century it was, according to a contemporary writer, "much frequented of people diseased with Lepre, Pokkes, Scabbes and great Aches."

Public hygiene was then on a low level, and when Queen Elizabeth I visited Bath in 1590, she was driven away by the stench of an open sewer. The 17th Century saw little improvement. Wrote one horrified historian: "All kinds of disorders were grown to their highest pitch. . . . The Baths were like so many bear gardens, and modesty was entirely shut out of them; people of both sexes bathing day and night naked; and dogs, cats, pigs and even human creatures were hurled into the water while people were bathing in it."

At this time Bath did not claim to be especially fashionable; there would have been little business for a portrait painter. But a great change began in 1702 when Britain's newly crowned Queen Anne and her consort, Prince George of Denmark, paid it a visit. The citizens cleaned up the town in preparation, and when the Queen arrived with a great company of lords and ladies, Bath gave her a spectacular welcome featuring two hundred girls dressed as Amazons. The royal party had a wonderful time. The Queen returned the next year with a glittering entourage; following an ancient custom, the town elected a "King of Bath," a Captain Webster, and made him Master of Ceremonies, responsible for the amenities of the second royal visit. The word then spread throughout England that Bath was the place where a person of fashion should be seen. Each year more of "the quality" came to "take the waters," and Captain Webster, who was a professional gambler, set up a lucrative gaming hall to exploit the rich visitors.

Other adventurers flocked to the feast, and among them was a remarkable person, an ambitious young Welshman named Richard Nash. He was not particularly handsome or dashing, but he was Oxford-educated, well dressed, had good manners, a pleasant wit and a way with women. In London he had lived off adoring women but in spite of manful efforts had not managed to capture a wealthy one as his wife. Coming to Bath in 1705 was a desperate venture; he had almost no money and only the elegant clothes he was wearing. Nash first tried gambling and honestly or dishonestly won £1,000. Then he charmed Captain Webster into making him his social assistant to deal with ladies and gentlemen of fashion while the captain attended to the hard-core gamblers. This arrangement worked very well, and when the captain was killed in a duel by a gambler who accused him of cheating, Nash became King of Bath and Master of Ceremonies in his place.

Beau Nash, as he was now called, turned into an inspired promoter and set about making Bath a center of wealth and fashion such as the world had never seen. He persuaded the city authorities to keep the town clean and get rid of the thieves and professional beggars who preyed on visitors. He ordered householders to hang out lanterns to light the streets and make them safe at night. His armed patrols drove robbers out of the town's suburbs, and his corps of inspectors regulated the prices and accommodations of the lodginghouses.

Even more important for the social future of Bath than his police measures was Nash's realization that his worst enemy was boredom. Bath had become suddenly fashionable because of the royal visits, and he knew that the nobility who flocked there would soon drift away unless they were continually entertained. He solved this problem in a characteristically 18th Century manner: by creating a round of social rituals that were considered compulsory for persons of importance.

Everyone who was anyone, from the grandest nobles and their ladies to the more elegant courtesans, rose at 6 a.m. and gathered at the hot baths, where they soaked, packed together, for an hour or so. Under the seemly regime of Beau Nash there was no public nakedness. The women wore garments of opaque, yellowish, canvaslike material that did not cling revealingly to the body when wet. Men also bathed fully clothed and usually wore their three-cornered hats. The sexes were supposed to keep separate, but opinions differ as to whether they did. According to Daniel Defoe, author of *Robinson Crusoe,* who describes one of the most fashionable baths: "the place being but narrow, they converse freely . . . make vows and sometimes love." The novelist Tobias Smollett told of "spectators in the galleries pleasing their roving fancies with bodies, faces, eyes, etc. In one corner stood an old lecher no less than 3 score years and 10 making love to a young lady not exceeding 14."

Following the ritual bath, the company assembled in the nearby Pump Room where everyone was expected to drink three glasses of warm, brackish and supposedly health-giving Bath water. They generally did so dutifully, but the Pump Room was more social than therapeutic. The ladies appeared in elaborate dishabille, their voluminous dressing gowns loosened to permit limited but intimate glimpses. Beau Nash also appeared, parading magnificently in a cream-colored three-cornered hat

Beau Nash, the renowned social director of Bath, is shown here in his prime, when the city's stylish visitors enjoyed the daily routine he had established but were careful to mind their manners lest they incur his displeasure. By the time Gainsborough arrived in town, Nash was living in shabby retirement. Antigambling laws had put an end to his days of glory, and for nearly two decades his fortunes steadily waned until his only income was a meager pension from the city he had helped make famous.

and a gold-frogged, lace-edged coat that he always wore open to show an embroidered waistcoat and ruffled shirt. Toying with a large gold or bejeweled snuffbox, he moved from group to group and was received with awe as if he were really a king. Women of the highest rank competed for his smile, and any deviation from what he considered good manners might provoke his frown, a social rebuke feared even by duchesses.

After the Pump Room came breakfast, which was often the occasion for elaborate private parties that were enlivened by "intruders," counterparts of the modern gate-crashers. Then came attendance at holy services in Bath's ancient and beautiful abbey, which has angels carved in stone climbing toward heaven up its façade. The services there were not deeply religious. The officiating clergy were notorious for obesity; one writer described them as "great overgrown dignitaries and rectors, with rubicund noses and gouty ankles, or broad faces, dragging along great swag bellies, the emblems of sloth and indigestion." No lowly people were admitted to these special rites; only the quality came, dressed in their gorgeous silks and satins, the women with towering headdresses, the men in powdered wigs. During the sermon the elderly slept while younger people flirted, the girls fluttering their painted fans and the young gentlemen sometimes passing amorous notes from pew to pew.

After the service the people might stroll around the town for a few hours, bowing to each other. They visited bookstores, which were places less for buying books than for sociability; women went to the dressmakers for lengthy fittings or browsed through the luxury shops that had moved from London to Bath. At 2 p.m. came an enormous midday dinner, followed by a promenade, tea in one of the suites of the building called the Assembly Rooms or an exchange of gossip in the Pump Room. On two nights a week there were formal dances in the Assembly Rooms. Beau Nash officiated, selecting couples of the highest rank to dance the first minuets while the rest of the company watched.

Today all this may sound boring, but many witnesses testify that for most 18th Century people it was not. English society was then rigidly aristocratic, and its titled folk got a feeling of grandeur merely from associating with one another. Lesser ranks, such as prosperous London merchants, also found Bath delightful because Beau Nash insisted that all visitors, if rich enough, must mingle freely in the streets and common rooms of his little kingdom. The merchants' families knew that when they returned to London the aristocrats whom they had met at Bath would cut them dead. But while they stayed in the magic city, they might talk with, even dance with, the haughtiest lords and ladies in the land.

Besides the official kinds of social intercourse, which included gambling, Bath had others. For the gentlemen's pleasure, the city was well provided with beautiful demimondaines, some of them well mannered and well dressed, and a good many of the titled ladies were eager for love affairs. Those who did not or could not enjoy such adventures could talk avidly about the indiscretions of others and find plenty of listeners. The gossip of the Pump Room was famous all over England for its matchless scandal and malice.

It took years for Beau Nash to get his solemn but enticing routine in

Prior Park, whose Neoclassical façade sprawls above, was the home of Gainsborough's wealthy friend Ralph Allen. At one time mayor of Bath and a dedicated booster of the city, Allen built his estate of the local limestone, called Bath stone, to show that it was ideal material for constructing a villa in the Palladian style then in vogue. To prove that Bath stone was weather-resistant too, he built Sham Castle *(top)*, a fake medieval ruin that consists only of a turreted wall, on the crest of a hill facing the town. Allen invited leading writers to visit Prior Park, and one of them, Henry Fielding, gratefully immortalized him as the benevolent Squire Allworthy of *Tom Jones.*

full operation, but he never faltered. As Britain prospered, more and more visitors came to Bath and spent more money there. Scruffy downtown blocks were rebuilt, and stately residential districts developed on the outskirts. Bath became what it is today, a city of Georgian mansions built of honey-colored Bath stone from quarries across the Avon.

When Tom Gainsborough settled in Bath in 1759, Beau Nash was in retirement (he died in 1761 at the age of 86), but the pleasure city he created had changed very little since his regime. Indeed it had become more prosperous and fashionable than ever, and its cultural level had risen. During the busy winter season, October to April, the leading actors and musicians of London now came to Bath to entertain its crowds of rich and titled visitors. Gainsborough in a sense was an entertainer too. As his friend Thicknesse had realized when he advised moving to Bath, a good many of the visitors were exceedingly vain. If the opportunity offered, they would pay a skillful young painter well to admire them, and perhaps make them immortal with his miracle-working brushes.

The antiquaries of modern Bath have argued earnestly about the place where Gainsborough first lived and painted in their city. The most reliable information says that he rented a big old house belonging to his sister, Mrs. Gibbon, the lodginghouse keeper. It was near Bath Abbey, where the fashionables gathered for their flirtatious worshiping, and was on a site now occupied by an annex to the present Pump Room. As a residence it could not have been pleasant. The air in the center of town was often thick with smoke from local soft coal burned in open fireplaces, and it was also steamy from the hot water of the baths. But the house had an all-important advantage: the room that Gainsborough used as his "painting room" faced the southwest door of the abbey. Every moneyed person who came to Bath was sure to pass the intriguing studio and perhaps step inside.

Mrs. Gibbon probably had a good deal to do with this canny selection of a studio, but in his biography of Gainsborough Thicknesse does not mention her. He says: "After his arrival at Bath, I accompanied him in search of lodgings, where a good painting room as to light, a proper access, etc. could be had, and upon our return to my house, where his wife was impatiently waiting the event, he told her he had seen lodgings of fifty pounds a year, in the churchyard, which he thought would answer his purpose. The poor woman, highly alarmed, fearing it must all come out of her annuity, exclaimed fifty pounds a year Mr. Gainsborough! why are you going to throw yourself into a gaol? But upon my telling her, if she did not approve of the lodgings at fifty pounds a year, he should take a house of an hundred and fifty, and that I would pay the rent if he could not, *Margaret's* alarms were moderated."

Thicknesse not only claims full credit for helping Gainsborough to get settled in Bath, but describes himself as the artist's first sitter there: "As at that time I was better known, and better loved at Bath, than I am at this, *though I am a very innocent* and *unoffending man, except to Rogues and Rascals.* My head was to be held up as the decoy duck, but the first sitting (not above fifteen minutes) is all that has ever been done to it, and in that state it hangs up in my house at this day; business came in so fast,

PHILIP THICKNESSE Efq.ʳ

A sour-faced Philip Thicknesse glares out of this satirical etching. Illustrating a biting criticism of Thicknesse' autobiography, the engraving is captioned with a quotation from Horace: "The man that maligns an honest friend, Roman, take care! His heart is black [of such a man beware]." Though he was warmly regarded by Gainsborough, Thicknesse had many enemies, and for good reason. He had once been jailed for libel; he tried to force a rich widow to marry him by encouraging a rumor that she was living with him; and he pitted his sons against each other by telling the younger that the elder had tried to kill him.

at five guineas a head, that . . . he was obliged to raise his price from five to eight guineas, and therefore I would not take up his time to finish mine. . . . It is scarce necessary to say how rapidly, nor how justly, he raised his price from eight guineas, till he fixed it at forty for a half-length, and an hundred for a full one."

Gainsborough's first portraits painted at Bath, those which brought five or eight guineas, were not particularly imaginative or creative. Perhaps he was overawed by his new surroundings, with Bath Abbey towering over his door and the people of quality strutting like peacocks in their silk and lace. But Tom was not a man to be impressed for long; he soon recovered his confidence and began to capture on canvas the essential nature of his sitters as brilliantly as he had at Ipswich. During the first year or so, most of his best work was portraits of oldish men whose strong characters he recorded with extraordinary vigor. His painting of Robert, Earl Nugent, done in 1760, is not merely the traditional "speaking likeness"; the earl seems about to rise from his chair and offer his hand with a smile.

For a while Gainsborough had few sitters among Bath's women of fashion; perhaps his growing renown as a painter of men kept them away. But Tom had not lost his love of women or his ability to portray them in a wonderfully attractive manner. While painting his elderly gentlemen, he also painted a charming young woman, Miss Ford, who was about to marry his friend Thicknesse. The work is lovingly treated, in a way that could be done only by a man who deeply appreciated beautiful women. Since Miss Ford was musically inclined, Gainsborough showed her with a viola da gamba and a guitar, and he placed her in a pose that was daring for its day. She leans slightly back against a table, her neckline is low, her legs are crossed, and the long curve of her thigh shows through the shimmering silk of her voluminous skirt.

Entitled *Mrs. Philip Thicknesse (page 127),* Miss Ford's portrait now hangs in the Cincinnati Art Museum, where its bold beauty stops visitors in their tracks, but when it was painted it found few open admirers. British society in the 18th Century was licentious but also extremely formal, and Mrs. Thicknesse' easy pose was considered shocking. A lady, Mrs. Delany, described her reaction to it in a letter to her sister, Mrs. Dewes: "This morning went with Lady Westmoreland to see Mr. Gainsborough's pictures. . . . There I saw Miss Ford's picture, a whole length with her guitar, a most extraordinary figure, handsome and bold; but I should be very sorry to have any one I loved be set forth in such a manner."

Modern eyes see nothing unseemly about *Mrs. Philip Thicknesse.* Instead they view the portrait as an illustration of Gainsborough's remarkable versatility. It is hard to believe that it was painted by the same man who so realistically painted *Robert, Earl Nugent,* and at about the same time. No doubt the portrait resembled the lady, but it is not a speaking, handshaking likeness, as is the earl's. It is far more: a poetic vision of beauty and pleasantly relaxed femininity.

Even while his portrait prices were still in the eight-guinea range, Gainsborough's volume of business made him prosperous enough to sublet his house near Bath Abbey and move out of the crowded center of town, where the smoky, steamy atmosphere had been bad for his health. In 1763 he wrote to his friend and attorney James Unwin: "I have taken a house about three quarters of a mile in the [Landsdown Road]; 'tis sweetly situated, and I have every convenience I could wish for; I pay 30 pounds per year; and so let off all my house in the smoake except my Painting Room and best parlor to show pictures in. Am I right to ease myself of as much painting work as the lodgings will bring in. I think the scheeme a good one."

The last sentences of this letter reflect Gainsborough's often-expressed dislike of portrait painting, on which his livelihood and reputation depended. Many portrait painters have felt this way, and the reason has been the same: their sitters generally think they are better looking than they really are, or at least have a view of themselves that clashes with the artist's. Although Gainsborough sometimes yielded grudgingly to the suggestions of his sitters or their families, he always resented having to do so and disliked paying humble respect to the arrogant noblemen who stalked into his painting room.

"Now damn Gentlemen," he wrote from Bath to a musician friend, William Jackson. "There is not such a set of enemies to a real artist in the world as they are, if not kept at a proper distance. *They* think (and so may you for a while) that they reward your merit by their Company & notice; but I, who blow away all the chaff & by G-- in their eyes too if they don't stand clear, know that they have but one part worth looking at, and that is their Purse; their Hearts are seldom near enough the right place to get a sight of it— If any gentleman comes to my House, my man asks them if they want me (provided they dont seem satisfied with seeing the Pictures) and then he askes *what* they would please to want with me; if they say a Picture, Sir please to walk this way and my Master will speak with you; but if they only want me to bow and compliment —Sir my Master is walk'd out—and so my dear there I nick them."

Tom did not, however, feel quite the same way about gentlewomen. His letter continues: "Now if a *Lady* a handsome Lady comes tis as much as his Life is worth [torn page] send them away so— But this is [torn page] as you knew this before—[torn page]"

The bits torn out of the pages are presumably the work of priggish Victorians who often bore down hard on Gainsborough's easygoing correspondence. A sizable collection of his letters written to Samuel Kilderbee—husband of the lady whose provocative portrait by Gainsborough now hangs in the Ipswich museum—is believed to have been destroyed entirely because of its "licencious language."

Gainsborough's new house in Landsdown Road was far enough from the center of Bath to give easy access to the countryside. Between his sessions of portrait painting, Tom took long excursions on foot or horseback, sketching rural scenes as he had done during his years in Sudbury and Ipswich. Often he had companions on these expeditions. One of them was a young man, Uvedale Price, whose later writings advocating admiration of England's natural beauty had a great effect on British esthetics. Price described the soothing effect that the countryside had on Gainsborough. "I often made excursions with him into the country around," he wrote.

"He was a man of eager, irritable mind, though he attached himself warmly to those he liked. Though of a lively and playful imagination yet was he at times severe and sarcastic, but when we have come near cottages and village scenes with groups of children, and objects of rural life that struck his fancy, I have observed his countenance to take an expression of gentleness and complacency."

Gainsborough had need for such therapeutic excursions, for his home life was becoming anything but pleasant. His wife, who had grown stout and was no longer pretty, had always been remarkably careful about money, and she did not become less so as her husband's prosperity increased. Instead, her concern for economy now came close to mania as she tried to block every nonessential expense.

Thicknesse gives an account of this unhappy situation: "Those who best loved Mr. Gainsborough, and whom he most loved, were unfortunately least welcome to his house, his table, or the good will of some part of his family; for he seldom had his own way, but when he was roused to exert a painful authority for it, and then he flew into irregularities, and sometimes into excess, for when he was once heated, either by passion, or wine, he continued unable and unwilling also, to do business at home, and at those times squandered away fifty times over, the money which an extra joint of meat, or a few bottles of port would have cost, to have entertained his friends *at home*. . . . Those who have sat to Mr. Gainsborough know that he stood, not *sat* at his Palate, and consequently . . . five or six hours work every morning, tired him exceedingly, and then . . . if he took a hackney coach to ease his tired limbs back again, he was obliged to be set down . . . out of the sight of his own windows, for fear of *another set down* not so convenient to his *head,* or his *heels,* as riding out twelve penny worth of coach hire, after having earned fifty guineas previously thereto! I have more than once been set down by him in that manner . . . and . . . been told *by him why we were so set down.*"

Besides his henpecking wife, Gainsborough had other domestic troubles, the greatest of which was his increasing worry about his two lovely daughters. In his portraits of them, their sad, unsmiling, timid look as young children became more pronounced as the girls grew older. A picture painted in 1763 or 1764 when they were in their teens shows them despondent, downcast, as if their tears were close to the surface. Only a devoted and worried father would show his daughters this way.

In Gainsborough's correspondence and in the works of his early biographers there are few references to his daughters, so few that the omission must have been deliberate. Apparently Gainsborough's friends and the men who first wrote about him knew something they did not want to admit. One friend wrote in a letter that according to the Gainsborough family physician the elder daughter, Margaret, was suffering from "a family complaint, and he did not suppose that she would ever recover her senses again." Margaret never married, and as she grew older she was mentioned as being eccentric to the verge of madness. Her sister, Mary, married against her father's will, separated from her husband and became truly insane, claiming to be a member of the Royal Family.

It is not surprising that Gainsborough's daughters were not normal people, living in a home disrupted by emotional conflict and surrounded by emotionally unstable relatives. Their mother's frequent allusions to her royal blood must have been a disturbing factor. Moreover, her extreme penuriousness was not quite rational. Also, Gainsborough's brother John (the man who invented metal wings and like King Bladud of Bath had tried to fly) was more than ordinarily eccentric. Gainsborough himself had fits of temper that made some of his friends occasionally doubt his sanity. Philip Thicknesse wrote: "I believe I may venture to say, that all great geniuses are a little allied to a kind of innocent madness, and there certainly was only a very thin membrane which kept this wonderful man within the pale of reason."

But Gainsborough certainly never broke through the "membrane"; he remained highly emotional but sane all his life. The chief effect of his unhappy home was to make him seek sociability elsewhere.

He does not seem to have looked often for that sociability in the endless round of Bath's artificial gaieties; he could not have done so much work if he had. But Bath offered the two things that next to painting he loved most: music and the nearby country. As he became prominent in local artistic circles, he got to know the leading musicians who lived in or visited Bath and soon made them his friends. He also admired theater people, and David Garrick, the most famous actor in England, became one of his intimates. Poets, novelists and other literary men came to Bath, but he avoided them. Only the playwright Richard Brinsley Sheridan was a close friend of his, and Gainsborough probably thought of Sheridan more as an actor than as a man of letters.

Another close friend of a different type was Walter Wiltshire, who ran a large fleet of coaches and freight wagons between Bath and London. The 18th Century equivalent of a railroad magnate, he had a country estate, Shockerwick, a few miles from Bath. Gainsborough often visited there, and Wiltshire gave him a fine gray horse to carry him to and fro. Gainsborough tried to pay him 50 guineas for the horse, but Wiltshire would not hear of any payment. So instead of money the painter sent him a marvelous and very personal landscape, *The Harvest Waggon (page 180)*, which is now considered one of his best. The two pretty girls on the wagon are his beloved and tragic daughters, and the gallant gray horse in the lead is the one that Wiltshire gave him.

Aside from his unhappy home life, Gainsborough's first few years in Bath seem to have been agreeable and amusing, and while he did many portraits he was not overworked. He was busiest at portrait painting during the winter social season; the rest of the year left time for country trips and merry parties with his musical or theatrical friends. But the longer he lived in Bath the more he was affected by what was then called "The Great World," the people of power, rank and wealth who streamed through the city. He could not help wanting to join The Great World as an important part of it, and he realized that to do so he must understand the aristocrats and provide what they wanted. So during the next stage of his career, he would deliberately train himself to paint in a manner that mightily pleased his noble customers, but which still left plenty of room for his love of poetry in painting.

Pleasures of Bath

For the pacesetters of Gainsborough's day the city of Bath was the place to go. Its natural attractions were mineral hot springs that gushed health-giving water at the rate of a half-million gallons a day. But it also lured the rich and aspiring with its open gambling and busy rounds of social events. To be accepted, visitors had only to obey the rules and behave democratically. In this tolerant atmosphere, people of all backgrounds mingled in a temporary suspension of England's rigid pecking order.

The bustling, lavish resort gave Gainsborough a golden opportunity to advance his name and his art. He began by painting portraits in small rented quarters. His work was so well received that in time his earnings from commissions enabled him to take a house in one of Bath's most exclusive and attractive enclaves. Indeed, as the photographs on these pages show, the entire city was —and is—an architectural gem.

But for all its grace and glitter, Bath had a tinge of the tawdry, a touch of the fraudulent. Its democratic exterior concealed a seething mass of snobbery, pretentiousness and intrigue. Its people and customs were easy prey for caricature. The frailties of Bath's habitués inspired the sketches done in 1798 by Thomas Rowlandson seen on the following pages, and also led the caustic Horace Walpole to remark that it did him 10 times as much good to leave the city as to go to it.

A view of Bath today, from the Abbey looking north, reveals the lingering charm of the city that for a century was a mecca for the fashionable English. It was extensively built up to accommodate visitors who wanted their own residences. Seen spread across the slope in the background, these elegant houses survive as a testament to an era of splendor.

The Concert

Assembly Room Ball

For the wealthy, the social demands at Bath could sometimes be trying; hordes of townspeople would gather in the Abbey yard *(right)* to gape at the expensively dressed visitors on their way to the daily church services that were a must. The women, weighted down under towering wigs and swaddled in yards of silk, were subjected to vulgar shouts of admiration and insulting suggestions. Safely inside the Abbey, the visitors were droned at by uninspired clergymen.

Evenings were devoted to concerts or balls held in the Assembly Rooms *(above)*. The first half of these dances was dominated by the courtly minuet, during which only one couple was allowed on the floor at a time. The tension of having to dance under the gaze of England's most prestigious people made "many fine women totter with fear," according to one observer. The second half of the evening featured country dances. Their liveliness, however, enraged at least one father. As his daughter was being whirled around, he "saw further above her shoe than I think fit" and whisked her from the floor.

Taking the Waters

The Pump Room

The express purpose of a stay at Bath was to "take the waters." The first thing in the morning, men dressed in jackets, drawers and tricornered hats, and women, also hatted and covered from head to foot in billowing linen coats, went to one of the city's baths, such as the elaborate Roman-style structure at right, and waded into the steaming mineral water whose temperature was more than 100°. Beside each lady bobbed a wooden dish that held her cosmetics and extra handkerchiefs to sop up the streams of perspiration from her face. The cleansing waters could barely penetrate the layers of clothes, but the bathers in any case were not keen on getting washed; they preferred to sweeten themselves with musky perfumes. Into the bath were also plunged scantily clad sufferers from such ailments as rheumatism, paralysis and skin disease. After this communal dip *(top),* the elite gathered in the Pump Room *(above)* to sip more of Bath's curative waters. Here gossip was exchanged at a furious rate, but the stories were usually so exaggerated that one titled lady said of the resort, "Nowhere so much scandal, nowhere so little sin."

A Party

The Portrait Painter

Portrait painting was big business at Bath. Vanity was in ample supply among the city's monied patrons, and they were happy to spend hours sitting for their pictures *(above)*. The demands on Gainsborough, in particular, were so great that after only seven years in the city he could afford a sumptuous home in the Circus *(right)*. This circular complex of stately houses was built in the Neoclassical tradition then popular, giving the effect of a Roman amphitheater.

While their elders pampered their own egos, the younger set at Bath indulged in other pastimes *(top)*. Young men trying to advance themselves by propitious marriages wooed the daughters of the privileged. The girls were alternately dealt or denied to eligible men like so much merchandise. Some of this trafficking took place at social functions that were highlighted by staggering meals of roast meats, fowl, fruits and heavy desserts, all washed down with sweet wines. One ironic result of such feasting was that many of the people who came to Bath to cure their gout found themselves with a new case of it—its telltale sign a bandaged foot resting gingerly on a cushion.

74

IV

Lords and
Lovely Ladies

In 1760, the year after Gainsborough moved to Bath, Britain crowned a new king, George III. He was not bright and not a good king, and his mismanagement caused Britain the loss of its American colonies. But he did have certain virtues. For one thing, he was British-born and British in outlook, not a transplanted German like his predecessors, George I and George II. He gave a good deal of attention and patronage to the arts, and this was also something new. Since James II, the last of the cultivated Stuart dynasty, lost his throne in 1688, no king had shown the slightest trace of artistic feeling. So the accession of George III serves as a handy date to mark the start of the classical age of British painting.

Actually, that golden age had already begun. Important Englishmen had long had their portraits painted—usually by a foreign artist—to hang in ancestral halls, but sitting for them had been a rather boring duty. Now, within little more than a decade, it had become both interesting and fashionable. Britain at last had painters who could make a lord look like a lord, and a lady look like a lady and also beautiful. A finished portrait need no longer depart at once for some remote country mansion, to be seen only by the family and a trickle of guests. Now many portraits remained in London to decorate town houses or to be displayed in the painter's exhibition room, which was open to visitors of the proper standing. Or they might be shown in a public exhibition where society came to appraise and admire. Having one's portrait painted by a famous British artist had become a social adventure. If the painting turned out well, it might make the sitter the talk of the town.

London's first large-scale and commercially successful exhibition of the works of native-born artists was held in 1760. In that year a loosely organized group of artists showed 130 pictures by 69 painters in a large room in the street near the Thames known as the Strand. Earlier showings of this sort had not been fully open to the public and were short-lived because they lacked dependable economic backing. But interest in painting had increased enormously. No admission was charged to the 1760 exhibition, but an illustrated catalogue sold so well at sixpence a copy that it paid all expenses and made the artists an unexpected profit of £100. Another exhibition was promptly scheduled for the next year.

Gainsborough was not among those whose works were shown in 1760, but he was well aware of this triumph of his colleagues, for the talk of London reached Bath quickly. During Bath's winter season the town entertained an important section of The Great World of London. The wealthy and titled people who visited Tom's studio under the tower of Bath Abbey, either to sit for portraits or merely to pass the time, were full of gossip about London. They knew that Lord So-and-so was sitting for a certain artist and was being portrayed as a Roman senator, or that Lady So-and-so had refused to accept a portrait because it made her nose too big. They also told about the success of the artists' exhibition in the Strand and named unknown painters whom it had publicized.

At first Tom listened with only mild interest. He was already more successful than he had ever expected to be, and London seemed far away. But as the lords and ladies dressed like birds of paradise trooped through his studio and praised his pictures, he began to think more about London and wondered what sort of an impression his work might make there.

So to the exhibition of 1761 Gainsborough sent a full-length portrait. It caused no recorded comment, but a portrait *(page 128)* submitted the next year won brief praise in the *St. James's Chronicle:* "Mr. Gainsborough. No. 30. A whole length of a Gentleman with a Gun. A good portrait and a Pleasing Likeness of Mr. Poyntz. The Dog well done."

The dog is indeed well done, and so is Mr. Poyntz. But for several years Tom's pictures made little further impression in London. In Bath there continued to be a lively market for his portraits, and many that he painted at this time rate as superlative in modern eyes. Well might he wonder at London's indifference and what he should do to attract the attention of the sophisticated capital. Perhaps the fact that he had never traveled abroad to study art counted against him. British painters had often looked to the Continent for their training and inspiration. Especially they had traveled to Italy to attend its famous academies and to study the works of the old masters. It must have occurred to Gainsborough that a pilgrimage to Italy might improve his standing in London, but with characteristic independence he made no move to follow the others.

The shining example of a British artist who had based his success on a visit to Italy was Joshua Reynolds, who by 1760 was already established as the most sought-after portrait painter in London. Born in 1723, he was four years older than Tom and came from precisely the same social background. His family were substantial burghers in the small town of Plympton, in Devonshire, on the southwest coast of England. His father was a clergyman-schoolmaster, like Tom's uncle, and other relatives were tradesmen in the town. Joshua was a serious, studious boy (no wandering in the woods or neglecting lessons for him), and when he was about 17 his father favored apprenticing him to a local apothecary.

Joshua had other ideas. For years he had been drawing, copying prints in his father's library and studying a book called *Essay on the Theory of Painting* by the British artist Jonathan Richardson, a work that fired his ambition to become a painter. At the age of 12 he had already painted a portrait of the Reverend Thomas Smart on sailcloth, using shipyard paints. It was not much of a portrait, but his father agreed that it showed talent. So when it came time to decide whether Joshua was to learn the apothecary's trade or seek a career in art, a well-to-do friend of the family, a Mr. Craunch, was called in to evaluate the boy's efforts and give his opinion. After due consideration Mr. Craunch thought that it might be arranged for one of London's best-known portrait painters, Thomas Hudson, to look at young Joshua's work. Hudson, whose many assistants and assembly-line methods enabled him to turn out competent likenesses by the dozen, was a native of Devonshire and often returned there to visit. If he saw promise in Joshua, perhaps he would take him on as an apprentice; in that event Mr. Craunch would pay for Reynolds' upkeep and training. Joshua was no doubt delighted, but his comment, as he remembered it later, was characteristically weighty. "I would rather be an apothecary," he said, "than an ordinary painter, but if I could be bound to an eminent master, I would choose the latter."

In this way Joshua Reynolds became a painter. In his own mind he soon saw himself as more than a painter, more indeed than a great painter. He would dedicate himself to the task of raising the prestige of British painters so that they would be accepted in aristocratic society, as leading men of letters already were. It was a large ambition for a young artist, but he never abandoned the goal, and to a remarkable extent he attained it.

In Hudson's "portrait factory" in London, where he entered a four-year apprenticeship, Joshua mastered the mechanical tricks of the trade so quickly that after about two years Hudson agreed to let him begin an independent career as a professional. Reynolds then left London to paint portraits at Plympton, but upon the death of his father in 1746 he set up housekeeping with his two unmarried sisters at Plymouth Dock, now Devonport. In making this move Joshua knew exactly what he was doing. To become a fashionable painter and raise his calling to high social status, he realized that he must make aristocratic friends, and Plymouth Dock, a Navy base, was a good place to begin. In those days nearly all British Navy officers belonged to the aristocracy.

For nearly three years Joshua worked doggedly, producing portraits that ranged from poor to good; the best were in no way extraordinary. He painted the local gentry and a good many naval officers, and his pleasant, earnest personality made many friends. But the big opportunity he was waiting for did not come until 1749 when a squadron commanded by a young nobleman, the Honorable Augustus Keppel, put into Plymouth to repair storm damage. Reynolds painted the commodore's portrait, which turned out to be the best he had done so far, and the two men became fast friends. When the squadron was seaworthy again, Keppel invited the artist to sail with him to the Mediterranean, where he was to persuade the pirate Dey of Algiers to leave British ships alone.

Reynolds left Keppel's ship at the Balearic island of Minorca, then a British stronghold. There he painted enough portraits to finance another step in the career he had planned for himself—a pilgrimage to Italy, the fountainhead of European art. He would study the old masters, especially Raphael. Then he would return to England and convince his countrymen that he could not only paint in the grand Italian manner but that he could

This portrait of the pudgy-faced Reverend Thomas Smart literally began as a thumbnail sketch—drawn on the end of young Joshua Reynolds' finger. Evidently bored by one of Smart's sermons, the 12-year-old surreptitiously made the sketch in church and then hurried to a boathouse retreat where, using marine paints and sail canvas, he painted the portrait. Normally a dutiful boy, Joshua had an occasionally overwhelming compulsion to draw and paint: his schoolmaster-father once came across his son's elaborately decorated Latin exercise and wrote on it, "This is drawn by Joshua in school out of sheer idleness."

do it more successfully than any of his British predecessors. He landed at Leghorn in January 1750 and headed for Rome, where he stayed for two years before visiting Florence, Bologna, Parma and Venice.

In Italy Reynolds did very little painting. He had not come to learn technique, which he felt he already knew. His program was analogous to that of the scholars of his period who read and reread Greek and Latin authors in order to stock their minds with apt quotations from Homer or Virgil and allusions to events in ancient history. He would cram his mind instead with images from Italy's glorious tradition of art. By spending hours in palaces and religious buildings where classical statues and paintings by the old masters were on display, Reynolds memorized faces, expressions, gestures, the arrangement of points of interest, and the uses of background light and shade to enhance the effect of figures in the foreground. But while saturating himself with the noble art of the past, he kept his opinions malleable, even allowing Michelangelo to replace Raphael as his idol. This showed independence because Raphael was at the time the most widely admired of the old masters.

No doubt Reynolds would have liked to return to England to paint famous scenes from the Bible or classical mythology, as the old masters had done. But he was a practical man, and he knew only too well that such "history pictures" by British artists would not sell. Wealthy Englishmen paid large sums for pictures in the grand Italian manner by Continental artists, but from native British painters they still bought almost nothing but portraits. Reynolds' plan, therefore, was to use his own adaptation of the grand Italian style of history painting in doing likenesses of English sitters. If his idea met with success, he hoped it would influence other British painters. Thus England's aristocrats might gradually come to recognize that native-born artists were capable of creating fine works other than portraits and accept them on a higher level. This may sound like too deliberate planning for an artist, but in Reynolds' mind and in the context of the 18th Century it was nobly motivated.

In 1753 Reynolds was back in London to put his carefully thought-out plan to the test. His first picture to attract public notice was a full-length portrait of his friend Commodore Keppel striding along a storm-lashed shore. It was no accident that the commodore's pose almost exactly duplicated that of the famous ancient Greek statue, the *Apollo Belvedere*. Nor was it an accident that the commodore's pose was almost identical to the one that Allan Ramsay—who was then the leading painter in London and who had also studied in Italy—used earlier for his well-known portrait of the Scottish chieftain Norman MacLeod of MacLeod. By painting a portrait similar to Ramsay's, Reynolds intended to demonstrate that he was the better artist, with a new and more vigorous way of bringing the grand Italian style to British portraiture.

He succeeded exactly as he had planned. *Augustus, Viscount Keppel (page 86)* won spectacular acclaim and put Reynolds in enormous demand as a portrait painter. Ramsay was toppled from his place as society's favorite portraitist. He revisited Italy in hope of regaining his primacy, but after he returned to England he gradually abandoned painting although he was quite as good an artist as Reynolds in many ways.

There is no doubt that of the two Apollo-based portraits Reynolds' is better than Ramsay's. MacLeod of MacLeod seems motionless; his facial expression lacks purpose and his outstretched hand is a weak gesture without meaning. Commodore Keppel, by contrast, is in purposeful motion. His face shows determination; his left hand grips the hilt of his sword and his right arm is extended in a gesture of firm command. He is heroic while MacLeod is not. Reynolds proved that by applying his version of the old masters' style to a classical model known to all educated Britons he could make his countrymen appear like glorious heroes.

By 1755 the demand for Reynolds' work was so great that he had painted more than 100 portraits. Not all were heroic or attempted to be; many were mere "heads," which cost less than a full-length likeness. But when Reynolds got a commission for a full-length portrait, especially when the sitter was a high-ranking nobleman, he usually painted him in a pose adapted from a well-known classical or Renaissance model.

Few people in 18th Century Britain regarded this practice of using the creations of the old masters to glorify English sitters as a form of artistic plagiarism. Indeed it was admired and applauded. While envious rivals of Reynolds sometimes whispered that he was making a fortune out of the concepts of other artists, the critics, connoisseurs and picture buyers did not see it that way. They agreed with Reynolds that he was naturalizing on British soil the noble tradition of the grand Italian style.

Reynolds was an astute businessman who missed few opportunities for self-promotion. Realizing that doting parents love to have their children's portraits painted, he made a special effort in this field. He was very good at it, especially in portraying little girls. His portrait of Lady Charlotte Fitzwilliam at the age of eight, painted in 1754, manages to be the picture of a delightful child and at the same time gives an impression of aristocratic loftiness. This was just what aristocratic parents wanted. From then on a good part of his practice was painting children. Although he remained a bachelor throughout his life, with no children of his own, he was thoroughly at home with them. He could make their eyes light up with mischief or merriment, or open wide with wonder.

His early success, before 1760, made Reynolds London's leading painter. He had brought to British painting a new versatility, but to his mind this was not enough. To accomplish the rest of his declared purpose of raising the social prestige of British painters, it would be necessary to set an example for them. Now he must make influential friends in the highest ranks and move conspicuously in the best society. As his fortunes improved, he advanced to successively larger houses where he could entertain impressively and he made a special effort to cultivate men of letters, who had already succeeded in elevating their social status.

His most important conquest was Dr. Samuel Johnson, the ponderous lexicographer, who wrote nothing that was widely read after his death but whose wit and learning made him the acknowledged ruler of London's literary life. Johnson was 14 years older than Reynolds, but the two became lifelong friends, and Reynolds often declared that Johnson was his source of wisdom and inspiration. Reynolds was a middle-class provincial with no formal education beyond his father's grammar school,

This mezzotint of Lady Charlotte Fitzwilliam was made from a portrait that Joshua Reynolds painted soon after his return from study in Italy. Although his subject was only eight and rather plain, he bedecked her in finery more suitable to a full-grown court beauty of the Renaissance, an indication of the impact of his Italian experience. Obviously, he was still liable to errors in taste, but his countrymen were impressed by the air of sophistication in the picture, and Reynolds quickly became a fashionable portraitist of children.

and Johnson's endless conversation, full of classical allusions and rolling, latinized sentences, was as good as an Oxford education. Other intimates of Reynolds included Oliver Goldsmith—poet, novelist and playwright—and Edmund Burke, a leading statesman as well as a man of letters. Encouraged and perhaps coached by his literary friends, Reynolds began to write articles on art and esthetics for the *Idler,* a literary magazine.

Business continued to flood into his studio. In order to handle the deluge—sometimes more than 150 portraits in a year—he employed a good deal of help. In the manner of Hudson, but never as mechanically, Reynolds planned and blocked out the portraits and painted the faces and other crucial parts himself. Under his watchful supervision his assistants did the rest, especially the clothes and backgrounds.

Shortly after the accession of George III, in 1760, Reynolds bought a large house in Leicester Fields (now Leicester Square), in the most fashionable part of London. He built a splendid gallery to show his pictures and kept his own carriage with all the necessary attendants. Wrote Dr. Johnson, who yearned for money but had little: "Reynolds is without a rival, and continues to add, as he deserves, thousands to thousands."

The mansion in Leicester Fields became one of London's leading intellectual and social centers. There Reynolds kept open house, limited, of course, to people of standing. While his sister Frances managed the housekeeping, he presided genially over the dinner table, where Dr. Johnson was often to be seen, eating gluttonously. To the house came the eminent statesmen of the day, the most famous writers, musicians and philosophers, the noblest aristocrats, the most dazzling beauties of society and the theater. Few painters came; although Reynolds had set himself up as a model for other British artists to emulate and was kind to artists in need of a helping hand, he never allowed himself to be close friends with a painter who seemed likely to become a rival.

Reynolds painted several portraits of his friend Samuel Johnson that were engraved and published as popular prints. This intimate study of the writer and lexicographer captures the intensity of the man. Dr. Johnson's own prose is often too turgid for modern taste, but he exerted tremendous influence over the other literary figures of his century through his writings and his brilliant conversation.

Perhaps Gainsborough was envious of Reynolds' fame and success but that does not seem likely. Money as such meant little to him; to the anguish of his pecunious wife, he spent it as soon as he got it. He did not hanker after Reynolds' social life; he disliked literary men and boasted that he never read books, and he rarely sought the company of titled folk. In one way, however, he may have envied Reynolds. Musicians and theater people, whose companionship was among Gainsborough's greatest delights, were both conspicuous in Reynolds' circle, and not many of the best ones stayed in Bath once the fashionable winter season ended. It may have been Gainsborough's love of music and the theater that made him think more and more about leaving Bath to plunge into the vortex of London. But before undertaking such a move, he knew that he must first develop a new style of portraiture, one that would make more of an impression on London's sophisticated art critics and picture buyers than his painting of Mr. Poyntz had done in the exhibition of 1762.

Gainsborough had already begun laying the foundation for this new style shortly after he settled in Bath in 1759. He must have soon learned that his most desirable potential sitters had enormous admiration for the stately portraits of English nobility by the great 17th Century artist Sir Anthony Van Dyck. Many of their families were proud possessors of

Van Dycks, or what they fondly believed to be Van Dycks, and they were not backward in comparing Gainsborough's work with that of the Flemish-born master. Therefore Gainsborough decided to make a conscious study of Van Dyck as a potential model for his own portraits of the aristocracy. Instead of going to Italy to absorb the old masters, as Reynolds had done, he would stay at home and study the single old master who had made the greatest impression on upper-class England.

Van Dyck was a unique phenomenon in the history of British painting. Born in Antwerp in 1599, he was a child prodigy, apprenticed at 11 to Hendrik van Balen, the leading painter of Antwerp, and accepted at 19 as a master in the Antwerp painters' guild. He visited England briefly in 1620 and painted for James I, the first of the Stuart kings, but left to study and paint in Italy. There, influenced chiefly by the works of Titian, he developed his matchless style of portraying aristocrats, depicting them in ways that subtly enhanced their elegance and grandeur.

When Van Dyck returned to England in 1632, he was already famous. Charles I, one of Europe's leading art connoisseurs, now sat on the throne, and he welcomed Van Dyck as no artist had ever been welcomed in England before. He gave him a London house, a gold chain and a medal, and made him a knight and "principalle Paynter in ordinary to their Majesties."

Possibly the King treated Van Dyck with such favor merely because he loved good painting, but there may have been another reason. Charles was in serious trouble with his people. In 1632 England was drifting toward civil war, and a principal cause was the King's insistence on governing as he alone saw fit. His supporters, the Cavaliers, were opposed by a faction, made up predominantly of commoners but including many noble and wealthy citizens, that claimed the King could not rule without Parliament's consent. Charles may have hoped to attract aristocrats and their followers away from the Parliamentarians by using Van Dyck's magic brush to create a romantic image of the Cavalier king.

In any case, that was what happened. With incredible speed Van Dyck turned out dozens of portraits of King Charles, his family and close associates. These were widely distributed in England and abroad, and they went far to create an impression that Charles was a handsome, romantic, wise and compassionate ruler beset by unpleasant, low-class factions among his subjects.

Van Dyck used all his skill to glorify the King. He showed him sometimes on horseback, sometimes standing imperiously, dressed in armor or in the gorgeous satins, ribbons and laces of the Cavalier period. The King was always tall, always gravely handsome, always an object for romantic worship. Actually he was not tall or particularly handsome, and his queen was not nearly as beautiful as Van Dyck showed her. Princess Sophia of Bavaria, who saw the English Queen when she visited Holland, wrote: "Van Dyck's handsome portraits had given me so fine an idea of the beauty of all English ladies, that I was surprised to find that the Queen, who looked so fine in painting, was a small woman raised up on her chair, with long skinny arms and teeth like defense works projecting from her mouth."

Samuel Johnson was such a well-known man about London that this cartoon of him dining with his young Scottish admirer, James Boswell, was simply titled "A Chop House"—the two figures were deemed instantly recognizable. Boswell's pose—too absorbed in his companion's talk to put fork to food—suggests that he was making mental notes for the great *Life of Samuel Johnson* he later wrote. Boswell also considered writing a biography of his good friend Sir Joshua Reynolds, but gave up the idea because he felt he knew too little about painting to do his subject justice.

Gainsborough particularly admired the 17th Century Flemish painter Anthony van Dyck, partly because he was a superb draftsman —as these portrait sketches show. Using incisive, sinuous lines, Van Dyck drew his teacher, Hendrik van Balen *(top)*, and the English architect Inigo Jones with a boldness of technique that is sometimes missing in his showy, highly refined painted portraits. And he gave these studies of his fellow artists greater psychological depth than he was often able to do when restricted by the expectations of his aristocratic sitters.

The same exalted treatment and sense of high purpose characterized many of Van Dyck's portraits of English noblemen. Imitators copied his style with varying degrees of success, and paintings in the Van Dyck manner saturated England and were exported to the Continent. They set the style of the glamorous Cavalier tradition, which lasted long after the Stuart kings had lost the throne. The Van Dyck mystique of what an elegant English nobleman should look like persists to this day.

Gainsborough's plan to remain in England and study Van Dyck, while easier than traveling to Italy to study other old masters, was not as easy as it may seem. Etchings and engravings of Van Dyck originals were sometimes available, but these could not provide the fine details that Gainsborough needed. The only way he could study Van Dyck with a searching artist's eye was to go where the paintings were, usually in the country mansions of the nobility. He is known to have visited several such houses in the vicinity of Bath, notably Wilton, the home of the Earl of Pembroke, who possessed a famous family group by Van Dyck. On increasingly frequent visits to London, Gainsborough also studied any Van Dycks that he could see there. He made sketches of them and sometimes painted careful copies.

Having filled his memory with Van Dyck, as Reynolds did with Italian old masters, Gainsborough proceeded to apply his knowledge, but he did it in his own manner. The portraits were not imitations of Van Dyck. They were lighter, less solemn. The men were more informal and the women were usually prettier. But they all had an aristocratic bearing and an elegance that no painter since Van Dyck had attained.

A particularly clear example of Gainsborough's adaptation of the Van Dyck style is his famous *Blue Boy (page 56)*, presumed to be a portrait of Master Jonathan Buttall. Although the boy was the son of a rich ironmonger, he wears a Cavalier's costume that seems more appropriate to Van Dyck's time than his own and he appears almost excessively elegant. Not all critics rate *The Blue Boy* among Gainsborough's great achievements, although it is undoubtedly his best-known work. Many think the picture's renown began with the legend that Gainsborough painted it as a challenge to Joshua Reynolds' remark that it was impossible to paint a really good portrait predominantly in tones of blue. The story, however, originated long after Gainsborough's death and, in any event, Reynolds himself had painted several excellent portraits in blue.

The change of Gainsborough's style is best seen in full-length portraits. A good example of Gainsborough's pre-Van Dyck style is the portrait of Mr. Poyntz, which had attracted only mild attention when exhibited in London. William Poyntz was a young man of the highest social stratum, and the picture was painted for his sister, Georgiana, Countess Spencer, but no symbols of rank or suggestion of rank are visible. Mr. Poyntz is leaning against a tree, his gun crooked in his arm and his dog at his feet. His clothes are simple and comfortable and his expression is mild, open, friendly. For all the picture shows, he might be the son of a minor squire or even a prosperous tradesman.

In sharp contrast is the portrait of Mrs. Graham *(page 131)*, painted some years later. Her clothes are rich, with layers of silks and laces. But she carries these symbols of wealth with grace and simplicity, as Van Dyck's aristocrats did. Moreover, Gainsborough makes Mrs. Graham appear tall, and tallness in the 18th Century was considered a noble attribute. With little in the painting by which to measure her true height, the best way to gauge it is to compare the length of her face with her total length. Seen thus, Mrs. Graham is quite tall. Her stature is more than nine times the length of her face. By contrast, Mr. Poyntz does not look especially tall because as Gainsborough painted him his stature is less than eight times the length of his face. Gainsborough often used this device to make his subjects look nobly tall, and he added to the apparent height of women by piling their hair high and narrowing their faces.

As soon as Gainsborough's new and elegant style appeared, his portraits began to make a much more favorable impression in London, and both his practice and prices in Bath increased. At the end of 1766 he was prosperous enough to move to the most fashionable address in that city of fashion: the Royal Circus. This circle of 33 stone houses embracing a park full of great trees survives as a masterpiece of Georgian architecture. Gainsborough probably lived in Number 17, two doors away from the Duke of Bedford, although a bronze plaque incorrectly placed on Number 24 in 1905 and never removed says he lived there.

The house at Number 17, which has five stories, looks large for Gainsborough, his wife and two daughters, but the 18th Century was a time of unabashed, almost required, ostentation, and a man was known not only by the size of his house but by the number of servants he kept. A number of these must have slept on the top floor and spent much of their time trooping up and down the stairs carrying food, water and coal.

All this sounds out of keeping with the character of Gainsborough, who had simple tastes and little regard for the figure he cut in society. He may indeed have selected the Royal Circus, in spite of his wife's resistance to spending money, because he felt he needed a conspicuous symbol to demonstrate his success and impress people who could afford to pay high prices for portraits. But there may have been another motive: the Circus is genuinely beautiful and Gainsborough, who loved beauty, may have felt pleasure in merely being there.

It was perhaps as well for his fortunes that he chose when he did to live in high style. Shortly after he moved to the Circus a long-planned project began to take shape in London—no less than the formation of the Royal Academy, made up of the leading artists in Britain, headed by Reynolds and sponsored by King George III. Gainsborough, whose new style of portraiture had by now made him almost as well-known and admired in London as he was in Bath, was invited to be one of the Academy's 36 original members, a position that carried valuable prestige. This honor might have come to him anyway, but on the other hand he was still something of an outsider. He had done no intriguing, as many of the other founding members had, and he possessed no powerful friends in artistic circles. So his residence in the famous Circus may have helped to convince the organizers of the Academy that even though this aloof and peculiar man was a provincial and a friend of none of them, they could not omit him from the list of founding Academicians.

Gainsborough's *The Blue Boy* was quite obviously painted in homage to Van Dyck, for it clearly follows the idea of the Flemish artist's portrait of the Villiers brothers *(above)*, foster sons of King Charles II. In a preliminary sketch for his painting *(top)*, Gainsborough combined the poses of Van Dyck's two boys to create the graceful stance of his own young subject.

The Gift for Portraiture

The world of 18th Century British art included a number of other luminaries besides Gainsborough. Allan Ramsay, a Scot, did portraits of such sensitivity that a contemporary critic described his work as "the furthest possible removed from anything like vulgarity." George Romney idealized his sitters with exquisite grace, and many lesser-known men also added luster to their country's art. But none of them was as fiercely dedicated to the cause of British painting as Sir Joshua Reynolds, the first president of the Royal Academy. Curiously enough, the snobbish and pompous Reynolds harbored a modesty about his own talent—and therein lay his strength. He began his career believing he was an average painter who could rise to greatness by studying classical artists and European masters and applying their themes, compositions, settings and even their costumes to portraiture. This conviction became the driving force in his crusade to link British painting, which had little tradition of its own, to important European art through the ages. It also fueled his own work; while striving to duplicate the grand manner of the past, he never stopped trying to improve as a painter. And his range of creativity suggests that he achieved excellence despite his theories rather than because of them. Toward the end of his life, he perhaps inadvertently revealed the true ambition that had dominated his brilliant career. In a letter to a friend he wrote, simply, "I have every year hoped to paint better."

A bachelor, Reynolds had a way with children, in person as well as on canvas—a quality apparent in his portrait of Lady Caroline Montagu-Scott, daughter of the Third Duke of Buccleuch. Believing that a portrait, to be true art, should be tied to allegory or an exalted theme, Reynolds represented the girl as "Winter."

Sir Joshua Reynolds: *Lady Caroline Scott as "Winter,"* 1776-1777

When Reynolds painted Commodore Keppel *(right)*, he did something entirely new in English portraits of men. Instead of merely creating a likeness, the usual practice, he cast his subject in a heroic mold. He put Keppel in a dramatic setting—a rocky shore after a shipwreck—and posed him with the stride and outstretched arm of the *Apollo Belvedere,* a celebrated classical statue he had seen in Italy. In his portrait of Lord Heathfield, Governor of Gibraltar *(far right),* Reynolds also elevated his sitter, this time by using symbolism, a favorite device of the old masters. Here the symbol is the key to the fortress chained to the governor's wrist; it proclaims that he will defend his command against all enemies.

Sir Joshua Reynolds: *Augustus, Viscount Keppel,* 1753-175

Sir Joshua Reynolds: *Lord Heathfield, Governor of Gibraltar*, 1787

Sir Joshua Reynolds: *Mrs. Siddons as the Tragic Muse*, 1789

Sir Joshua Reynolds: *Three Ladies Adorning a Term of Hymen (The Montgomery Sisters)*, 1774

Reynolds, who painted his men in heroic attitudes, often cast his women in mythological roles: an actress as the tragic muse, three young ladies as attendants to a Greek god.

In the picture above, he encountered a certain awkwardness in clothing the daughters of Sir William Montgomery in myth. They appear adorning the altar of Hymen, the god of marriage. But since only two of the sisters were married, Reynolds put the third girl, at the left, in the position of a helper.

No such problem arose when he portrayed the famous actress Sarah Siddons. An accomplished tragedienne, Mrs. Siddons was able to appear both elegant and comfortable as the tragic muse. She sits on a throne in an attitude that Reynolds borrowed from Michelangelo's Prophet Joel in the Sistine Chapel; the shadowy allegorical figures of Pity and Terror, lurking behind her, add to the theatrical quality of the portrait. After he finished it, Reynolds humbly confessed to the great lady, "I would not lose the honor this opportunity offered to me of going down to posterity on the hem of your garment," and signed his name on the edge of Mrs. Siddons' voluminous skirt.

Sir Joshua Reynolds: *Georgiana, Countess Spencer with Lady Georgiana Spencer*, 1759-1761

Sir Joshua Reynolds: *The Duchess of Devonshire and Lady Georgiana Cavendish*, 1784

Reynolds yearned for entree into England's high society—and he gained it, in large part, by painting its members beautifully. But even while catering to their conceits, he continued to search for effective styles. The pair of mother-and-daughter portraits at the right illustrate two of his approaches. He depicted Georgiana, Countess Spencer and her daughter *(above)* in a composition suggesting a Renaissance Madonna and Child. When a generation passed and it was time to paint the daughter, also named Georgiana and now the Duchess of Devonshire, with her own child, Reynolds did not repeat the style of the earlier portrait. Instead, he painted the vivacious Duchess in an attitude of charming play.

In the most ambitious commission he ever received, a painting of the family of the Duke of Marlborough, Reynolds demonstrated still another style. The classicizing formality he gave this monumental group portrait is readily apparent in the studied placement of each child, in the Duchess' pose against a mock Greek ruin and in the emphatic nobility of the seated Duke.

George DUKE of MARLBOROUGH—Caroline D.^s of MARLBOROUGH—George MARQUIS of BLANDFORD—LORD Henry Spencer—LADY Caroline Spencer—LADY Eliz.th Spencer—LADY Charlotte Spencer—LADY Anne Spencer.

PAINTED By Sir Joshua REYNOLDS. 1778.

Sir Joshua Reynolds: *The Fourth Duke and Duchess with Their Family*, c. 1778

Allan Ramsay: *The Painter's Wife (Margaret Lindsay)*, c. 1755

George Romney: *Sir Christopher and Lady Sykes*, 1786

Natural Grace and Skillful Flattery

Among the gifted artists who shared the world of Reynolds and Gainsborough were Allan Ramsay and George Romney. The pale gown and glimmering laces in Ramsay's portrait of his wife, Margaret *(far left)*, show his delicate touch as a colorist; the tenderness of her expression, the lifted hand, illustrate the personal warmth with which he infused his work.

Romney, who portrayed Sir Christopher and Lady Sykes *(left)*, was a cabinetmaker's son who tended to equate portraiture with constructing a handsome piece of furniture. His work reveals no secrets of personality or character in his subjects. He simply made them appear elegant and aristocratic, a form of flattery no one could object to.

93

Lady Hamilton Reading a Newspaper, c. 1783

Lady Hamilton as "Nature," 1782

Lady Hamilton as Circe, c. 1782

Lady Hamilton as a Bacchante, c. 1786

At the age of 48, Romney, long separated from his wife and two children, fell in love with Emma Hart, a dainty, dark-eyed girl of about 19, who represented the ideal beauty he had always wanted to paint. She was brought to Romney's studio in London by her protector, the Honorable Charles Francis Greville, who, after the fashion of the time, wanted his mistress immortalized by a popular painter. From 1782 to 1786 Romney celebrated Emma's perfection, as he saw it, in hundreds of sketches and drawings and some 30 finished portraits, eight of

Lady Hamilton at Prayer, c. 1782-1786

Lady Hamilton as Ariadne, c. 1785

Lady Hamilton at the Spinning Wheel, 1782-1786

Lady Hamilton as Cassandra, c. 1785-1786

which appear here. Emma was a good model for a painter who did not look beyond appearances. A Welsh country girl, she had been taught by the fastidious Greville to imitate the habits and attitudes of a lady: her demure manner was as artificial as the allegorical poses she assumed for the artist. Romney perpetuated Emma's natural beauty on canvas. But she won a larger place in history after she married the somewhat senile Sir William Hamilton and became the mistress of England's great naval hero Lord Horatio Nelson.

V

Reynolds' Society
of Artists

The founding of the Royal Academy was a triumph of social and political intrigue, the 18th Century's favorite way of getting things done. A royally sponsored academy devoted to the improvement of British art had long been discussed. Other countries, notably France, had such useful and decorative institutions; why not Britain too? But during the time of King George II, who reigned until 1760, the Crown showed no interest in art. In fact the King was antagonistic. He is recorded as saying in his thick German accent, "I hate *b*ainting and *b*oetry too!" When he saw an engraving of one of Hogarth's earthy pictures, which shows raffish soldiers reluctantly kissing their girls goodbye, he flew into a rage. "What! A *b*ainter burlesque a soldier? He deserves to be picketed [tortured] for his insolence. Take his trumpery out of my sight."

Still, the idea of an art academy backed by the Crown persisted. In 1755 a distinguished committee including Francis Hayman, Gainsborough's teacher and boon companion during his early, roistering years in London, and Joshua Reynolds, who was then in the first flush of his fame, had already drawn up an elaborate plan to establish a royal academy. It received no royal support or approval, and the artists had no money to proceed alone. An attempt was made to enlist the help of the Society of Dilettanti, a group of rich and titled connoisseurs, but these gentlemen would not open their purses without a guarantee of ultimate control, which the artists would not give.

So matters stood until 1760, when the artists held their pioneer exhibition in a room in the Strand owned by the Society of Arts—whose full, resounding name was The Society of Arts for the Encouragement of Arts, Manufactures and Commerce—and actually made money by selling 6,582 catalogues at sixpence apiece. The triumph was marred by a few unseemly occurrences; since admission was free, a considerable number of unruly persons crowded into the exhibition and lowered the tone of the company. But the unexpected popularity of the show and its even more unexpected profit were a bright inspiration to the artists, who now saw a way to show their pictures to a large and moneyed public at no cost to themselves.

The prospects looked so good, in fact, that bitter quarrels broke out among the artists over who should exhibit and how pictures should be selected. They split into two groups. A faction calling itself the Free Society of Artists continued to exhibit in the Strand but soon lost importance. The other faction, to which Reynolds and most of the better artists belonged, took the title of Society of Artists of Great Britain and exhibited in 1761 in new quarters. One shilling was charged for a season ticket, which thinned out the crowds of visitors and improved their quality.

From the start the Society of Artists began laying plans to win the patronage of King George III, who had come to the throne in 1760 and was more friendly toward art than his churlish predecessor. For the catalogue of its 1761 exhibition it persuaded Hogarth, now semiretired, to contribute two engravings. The one used as a frontispiece showed a bust of King George benevolently watching Britannia as she waters three flourishing saplings labeled *Painting, Sculpture* and *Architecture*. The tailpiece showed a foppishly dressed monkey watering three dead stumps marked *Exoticks*. This opportunity to give vent to his hatred of foreign artists must have pleased Hogarth and may have been the reason he consented to supply the illustrations. In another move to flatter King George, the Society invested more than £50 of its meager funds to fire rockets and illuminate the front of its exhibition quarters on the King's birthday.

This strategy began to bear fruit in 1765, when the Society obtained a rather meaningless royal charter and changed its name to The Incorporated Society of Artists of Great Britain. It now had a membership of more than 200 and was holding elaborate banquets to celebrate its growing importance. But quarrels among its loosely organized members never ceased. They became worse until, in 1768, most of the leading directors, Reynolds included, resigned on the ground that certain members who were more interested in business than in art were using the Society for their own commercial advantage.

Gainsborough, still living in Bath in 1768, was well acquainted with the dissension that had split the Society, for the man who had the misfortune to become its president at this critical time was Joshua Kirby, an intimate friend of his since their Ipswich days. Kirby had moved to London, where, despite his humble background as house painter and picture dealer, he had won recognition in the city's artistic circle for a book he had written on perspective and also because he had tutored the King in that subject. Kirby, who was not among the Society's members accused of misbehavior and who had the best interests of the Society at heart, asked Gainsborough to replace one of the resigned directors. Gainsborough refused; officeholding of any kind was alien to his nature. Also, he was aware that the Society's seceding faction had been waging a clandestine campaign to persuade King George to sponsor an official, tightly organized art academy under its exclusive control. Reynolds had written Gainsborough asking him to become one of the original members if such an academy materialized.

Reynolds himself played no obvious role in all this intrigue. Overt leadership was left to others, among them Benjamin West, a rising young Pennsylvania-born painter who had settled in England, and William

When asked by the newly founded Society of Artists to illustrate its exhibition catalogue in 1761, Hogarth took the opportunity to vent his prejudice against foreign art with this caricature of an art connoisseur: a richly dressed monkey enthusiastically watering three dead plants labeled "Exoticks." The symbolism indicated Hogarth's contempt for the wealthy collector who, blind to the merits of talented native English painters, worshiped traditional imported art solely for its antiquity or exotic qualities.

Chambers, who held the position of royal architect. During long, private audiences with the King, they managed to convince him of the wisdom of founding a royal academy to rival that of France. So that Kirby and his faction would not get wind of their conversations, the King insisted on the strictest privacy.

In an atmosphere of conspiracy, hush-hush meetings in the plotters' homes and worshipful conferences in the Presence, the artists and the young monarch agreed on the academy's plan of organization. In his own hand George III wrote some of the bylaws; most of the rest were taken from the abortive proposal drawn up under Hayman and Reynolds in 1755. The new plan was set forth in a formal document that needed only the King's signature when suddenly the artists were faced with a grave dilemma.

A meeting had been called at the home of one of the artists to discuss details of the project, which was now certain of the King's support, and to the dismay of all it was learned that the all-important Reynolds would not attend. While the meeting waited with bated breath, West hurried off to plead with Reynolds, who claimed to be "much surprised matters were so far advanced."

To be sure, Reynolds had taken no visible part in the negotiations with King George; in fact he took a trip to France during a crucial period. But it is hard to believe that he was not involved. An academy with the full prestige of the Royal Family behind it would advance his life-long ambition to raise the social status of British artists, and his carefully nurtured social life provided him with high-placed friends to plead the cause at court. An inherently cautious man, he may have refused to join the meeting and openly identify himself with its plotting until he had last-minute assurance that the King would sign the academy into being.

In any case, it took West two hours to persuade Reynolds to accompany him to the meeting. The members were about to disperse, but when Reynolds entered they rose and with one voice acclaimed him as "president" of the nascent academy. A few days later, on December 10, 1768, the King signed the Instrument of Foundation of the Royal Academy, and the long-dreamed-of institution was at last a reality. Reynolds had achieved one of his ambitious goals and the following year he attained another—he was knighted by the King.

The Academy's Instrument of Foundation aimed at a strong central organization and an end to disorderly bickering. It declared that only painters, sculptors or architects of high moral character and eminence in their profession could be elected members (called Royal Academicians) and that their number should be no more than 40. The powers of officers were defined, and minute details were taken care of down to the salary of the sweeper, £10 per year. The Instrument's most important phrase, however, was in the preamble, in which the King declared himself the Academy's "patron, protector and supporter." The artist-promoters had promised that the Academy would strive to be self-supporting, but it was understood that the King would come to its aid in a financial crisis and would also provide quarters for its art schools and exhibitions. George III and his successors lived up to these obligations with increasing magnificence, giving the Academy the home and security of a favored government institution, which it retains to this day. From its first modest home in London's Pall Mall, it moved to successively larger and more elegant quarters, and a century after its founding it became housed in its present complex of stately buildings in Piccadilly.

For their part, the Academicians agreed to teach young painters, sculptors and architects free of tuition. By the end of the Academy's first year there were 77 students; Dr. William Hunter, the popular professor of anatomy, used as models both living persons and the bodies of criminals who had been hanged, and of these there was no lack in the 18th Century. Female models, especially nude ones, presented a problem of propriety. The solution was a rule stipulating that "no Student under the Age of twenty, be admitted to draw after the Female Model, unless he be a married Man," and that "no Person (the Royal Family excepted) be admitted . . . during the time the Female Model is sitting."

Almost at once the Royal Academy became the focus of British artistic life. At its first General Assembly, President Reynolds—thereafter called simply "the President" by his associates—read a polished address that set the official tone for Britain's classical age of painting. Such "Discourses," which Reynolds was to deliver annually or biennially for the rest of his life, were not always consistent within themselves. Neither were they wholly consistent with Reynolds' own practice. They could hardly be so, since they spanned half of the career of a many-sided man who never stopped growing creatively.

The Discourses are, nevertheless, an extraordinary performance. They are written in a measured, rolling style that Reynolds undoubtedly learned from his friend Dr. Johnson, and they match the mood of their period. The 18th Century, in Britain particularly, was a time of vigorous growth, innovation and disorder, but it saw itself as a judicious "Age of Reason." Overlaying its fundamental change and turmoil was a thin, brittle skin of decorum, devotion to the classical past, and respect for moral systems constructed by the mind, not by the emotions. Reynolds epitomized those qualities; his Discourses are the perfect expression of 18th Century thought as applied to artistic practice and criticism.

In his first Discourse Reynolds urged the Academy's students, as beginners, to learn how to make precise drawings. "He who endeavors to copy nicely the figure before him, not only acquires a habit of exactness and precision, but is continually advancing in his knowledge of the human figure, and though he seems to superficial observers to make a slower progress, he will be found at last capable of adding (without running into capricious wildness) that grace and beauty, which is necessary to be given to his more finished works, and which cannot be got by the moderns, as it was not acquired by the ancients, but by an attentive and well compared study of the human form."

To this sound, if conventional, counsel Reynolds added some moral advice, including the questionable statement: "When we read the lives of the most eminent painters, every page informs us that no part of their time was spent in dissipation." But Sir Joshua was not primarily concerned with the technical training and morality of art students. His dominant theme was the high purpose of art: to elevate and improve, not merely to please or entertain. To reach this lofty level, he said, the young artist should read the poets and cultivate men of learning. "Reading, if it can be made the favourite recreation of his leisure hours, will improve and enlarge his mind, without retarding his actual industry. What such partial and desultory reading cannot afford, may be supplied by the conversation of learned and ingenious men, which is the best of all substitutes for those who have not the means or opportunities of deep study. There are many such men in this age; and they will be pleased with communicating their ideas to artists, when they see them curious and docile, if they are treated with that respect and deference which is so justly their due."

At no time should the artist depend on his "genius." Reynolds used the word "genius" in various senses, usually to deny that it exists. In his second Discourse he is most specific: "There is one precept, however, in which I shall only be opposed by the vain, the ignorant, and the idle. I am not afraid that I shall repeat it too often. You must have no dependence on your own genius. If you have great talents, industry will improve them; if you have but moderate abilities, industry will supply their deficiency. Nothing is denied to well-directed labour: nothing is to be obtained without it. Not to enter into metaphysical discussions on the nature or essence of genius, I will venture to assert, that assiduity unabated by difficulty, and a disposition eagerly directed to the object of its pursuit, will produce effects similar to those which some call the result of *natural powers.*"

Young artists, said Reynolds, after learning to draw exactly, and stocking their minds with literature, should set their sights on the highest ideal of painting. This, he stated repeatedly, is not mere representation of nature, however skillfully done, nor is it an expression of the artist's personality, however gifted he may consider himself to be. It is the search for perfect beauty, guided by the old masters of classical times and the Renaissance, and inspired by the noblest poets and philosophers.

Nature is full of imperfections, Reynolds explained; no human face or figure is ideal. So the task of the artist is to eliminate flaws, disproportions and departures from the norm. Only when he has become skilled at such purification can he create true beauty. There must be some variation, of course. Children should not be made to look like adults, and a Hercules should not be given the same physique as an Apollo. But in each case there is an ideal "central form" that should be sought diligently.

"This idea of the perfect state of nature," said Sir Joshua, "which the artist calls the ideal beauty, is the great leading principle, by which works of genius are conducted. By this Phidias acquired his fame. He wrought upon a sober principle; what has so much excited the enthusiasm of the world; and by this method you, who have courage to tread the same path, may acquire equal reputation." Seeming to realize that his prescription for winnowing ideal beauty out of nature's errors was beyond the ability of many painters, Reynolds pointed out an easier path to the same objective. "I know but of one method of shortening the road; this is, by a careful study of the works of the ancient sculptors; who, being indefatigable in the school of nature, have left models of that perfect

George III, the first of the Hanoverian kings to show an interest in art, struck an energetic stance for this silhouette, cut by his daughter Elizabeth. The King had 15 children, a record for a British monarch, and he was so closely attached to his six daughters that he consented to their marriages only with difficulty. Elizabeth, the third girl, began to draw as a child and was nicknamed "The Muse." When she was 25 she designed a series of engravings on "The Birth and Triumph of Cupid," which her father proudly published at his own expense.

In 1771 King George III provided quarters for the Royal Academy in Somerset House —seen on the right in the engraving above —a palace that the Crown had owned since the 16th Century. Its façade, though "open to the most frequented street in London," was unfortunately narrow, but the architect who remodeled the building, Sir William Chambers, used an austere Neoclassic style and decorative sculpture to create an imposing yet pleasing entrance. To gain more space the Academy moved in 1868 to Burlington House, shown below as it was in its original state in the 17th Century, a country mansion set off by formal gardens in what were then the outskirts of London.

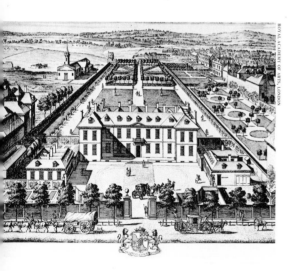

form behind them, which an artist would prefer as supremely beautiful."

So much for the method of achieving true beauty, but how should an artist select his subject? Reynolds was equally specific on this point. "The painters who have applied themselves to low and vulgar characters . . . (such as we see in the works of Hogarth) deserve great praise; but as their genius has been employed on low and confined subjects, the praise which we give must be as limited as its object." Even lower in his opinion were battle pieces, pictures of animals, "the French gallantries of Watteau," landscapes and sea views. Lowest of all among artists in Reynolds' estimation were those who aspired to nothing higher than the painting of "cold" portraits and of still life. He had a few kind words for even such men, but his condescension was louder than his kindness.

For artists to raise their painting to a sublime level, he explained, they must limit themselves to exalted themes. "Invention in painting does not imply invention of the subject; for that is commonly supplied by the poet or historian. . . . Such are the great events of Greek and Roman fable and history, which early education and the usual course of reading, have made familiar and interesting to all Europe, without being degraded by the vulgarism of ordinary life in any country. Such too are the capital subjects of scripture history, which, besides their general notoriety, become venerable by their connection with our religion."

Paintings that lack such grand subjects Reynolds ranked as merely "ornamental." The great Dutch and Flemish masters of the 16th and 17th Centuries he considered devotees of this ornamental style, and also most of the Venetians of the Renaissance, excepting Titian. Their subjects were taken from their own times, and their figures and settings have individual character, not "ideal beauty." Reynolds realized clearly, however, that many kinds of painting (notably portraiture, his own specialty) could not always meet the criteria of the grand style he advocated. So he reduced to some extent the rigor of his doctrine and admitted that artists who understood the principles of grandeur could elevate and ennoble even the lower ranks of painting.

Often in his Discourses Sir Joshua referred to the touchy subject of imitation, which he had been accused of practicing too assiduously. "Let it be observed," he pointed out, "that a painter must not only be of necessity an imitator of the works of nature . . . but he must be as necessarily an imitator of the works of other painters: this appears more humiliating, but is equally true; and no man can be an artist, whatever he may suppose, upon any other terms . . . the study of other masters, which I here call imitation, may be extended throughout our whole lives, without any danger of the inconveniences with which it is charged, of enfeebling the mind, or preventing us from giving that original air which every work undoubtedly ought always to have."

Though Reynolds did not originate these classicist ideas, he expressed them more clearly than anyone else, and he did so with a definite purpose. In laying down his principles he hoped to create in Britain a notable school of "history painting." He believed that this was the only way by which British painting could be raised above the status of a skilled mechanical trade. He did not always follow his own rules; indeed, he could not, since the market for history pictures by native-born artists was extremely limited, and no one knew it better than he. His Discourses were therefore intended to increase that market by convincing wealthy Englishmen that they should appreciate and commission such works.

In a limited and partial way he succeeded. During the first period of his career, from about 1755 to 1765, he had often painted his sitters in poses based on classical models, as he did Commodore Keppel, but he also strove for accurate likenesses, which meant retaining "nature's errors" —their personal characteristics. He allowed them to dress in contemporary clothes, another thing he deplored, and made no attempt to involve them in episodes from mythology, ancient history or the Bible. It is safe to say that most of the sitters would have resisted if he had tried at this stage to do otherwise.

Many portraits of this period are among Reynolds' best; to some tastes they are the best he ever did. Perhaps the most charming of them is *Georgiana, Countess Spencer with Lady Georgiana Spencer (page 90)*, painted about 1761. The pose is that of a Renaissance Madonna and Child, but the lovely young countess and her little daughter are individuals. They are touchingly human, affectionate and alive, and their faces show character in a wonderfully delicate way. No ancient sculptor or poet told Sir Joshua how to paint them.

This tender picture and others in the same style do not follow Reynolds' own rules for achieving the grand manner. But even before he delivered his Discourses, he was painting pictures that, while ostensibly portraits of individuals, were nevertheless closer to his ideal of "history painting." He began to dress some of his sitters in long, loose robes resembling those of classical times instead of in the intricate silks and laces of 18th Century fashion, and he made their faces less individual and more "ideal."

In 1765 he persuaded Lady Sarah Bunbury to be portrayed as a woman of classical Greece offering a sacrifice before an altar topped by marble statues of the Three Graces. Lady Bunbury was only 20 at the time but, bundled in heavy robes that conceal her figure, she looks quite matronly. It is possible that her face is a true likeness, but it has no character or individuality. It is more like the face of a Greek statue and shows Reynolds' version of the ideal beauty so highly praised in his Discourses.

A few pictures of this same type were more successful, perhaps because the sitters provided more inspiration than did Lady Bunbury. For instance, when Reynolds painted the Honorable Mrs. Peter Beckford sacrificing to Hygeia, the Greek goddess of health, her tragic expression together with the gloomy setting give the picture a powerful emotional appeal. Reynolds undoubtedly knew that Mrs. Beckford, a famous London beauty, had reasons to look tragic. She was tubercular (hence the altar of Hygeia), unhappily married and the mistress of her husband's cousin, William Beckford. Even in licentious 18th Century London this liaison outraged society. William Beckford and his beautiful mistress both became enamored of the 11-year-old son of Viscount Courtney, and the threesome stirred additional scandal by participating in Black Masses and other nefarious rites. Perhaps Reynolds was too proper to pay at-

These allegorical mural paintings were made for the ceiling at the Royal Academy's Somerset House by Benjamin West. The center panel, *The Graces Unveiling Nature*, is surrounded by female figures representing the four elements—Earth, Air, Water and Fire. West was a poor but ambitious country boy from Pennsylvania who had studied art in Italy before coming to London to make a career. He had been taught to paint from antique statues rather than live models, and the sculptural quality of these idealized nudes reflects his Italian training. He later served two terms as president of the Royal Academy and never returned to America.

tention to all these sordid details, but he showed with his brush that all was not well with the Honorable Mrs. Peter Beckford.

Reynolds seldom persuaded his male sitters to dress in anything but contemporary clothes, but as time passed, more and more of his female subjects wore "Grecian" clothes and were posed doing vaguely Grecian things. The most ambitious of these classicized portraits, painted in 1774, is *Three Ladies Adorning a Term of Hymen (page 89)*. The painting shows three daughters of the Scottish jurist and Member of Parliament Sir Williams Montgomery about to drape a garland of flowers on a bust of Hymen, the Greek god of marriage, that stands on a tapered column known architecturally as a "term."

The girls were famous both as beauties and as amateur actresses, and the fiancé of one of them, Luke Gardiner, had written to Sir Joshua in courtly prose: "This letter will be delivered to you by Miss Montgomery, who intends to sit to you with her two sisters, to compose a picture, of which I am to have the honour of being the possessor. I wish to have their portraits together in full length, representing some emblematic or historical subject; the idea of which, and the attitudes which will best suit their forms, cannot be so well imagined as by one who has so eminently distinguished himself by his genius and poetic invention."

To Reynolds this was a golden opportunity: three beautiful, famous and highborn models ready to pose for a picture conforming exactly to his concept of the grand manner. He gave the commission his closest attention, digging deep into his sketch books for helpful suggestions from the old masters and no doubt asking his learned friends for nuggets of inspiration from classical literature. The theme he selected had its origin in the Greece of ancient times, when women wanting children offered sacrifices to Priapus, the erotic god of fertility. Later ages discarded Priapus in favor of Hymen, the god of lawful wedlock. Many old masters had used variations of the theme, among them Nicolas Poussin, who painted a riot of lightly clad nymphs dancing a wild bacchanal before the god, and Peter Paul Rubens, who made his three worshipers as voluptuously nude as only he could.

Reynolds, of course, had no such indecorous plan; he was dealing with the respectable daughters of a Scottish Member of Parliament. After examining the precedents like a lawyer tracing a land title, he finally posed the girls in a balanced pattern that was a composite of many earlier pictures and in accordance with his principles. There is even a bit of symbolism decipherable only by the girls' families or intimate friends. Since two of them were married by the time they posed for Reynolds, he painted them actually draping the garland on Hymen; the still unmarried sister is shown gathering flowers to win the god's favor.

There is something wonderful about this picture and also something ridiculous. All its details, including an incongruous Oriental rug on which one of the girls is kneeling, confirm Sir Joshua's great skill with the brush. Yet he was trying to do the impossible: to paint a picture of a classical theme in the grand manner and still conform to the conventions of his own time. Though the girls represent the Three Graces, whom Greek and Renaissance artists customarily portrayed with no clothes at all, they are wearing voluminous pseudoclassical robes that reveal only blunted outlines of their bodies. They are posed in a tableau with no suggestion of movement, and although their faces have some of the "ideal" beauty of Greek statues, they are utterly serious and proper, with none of the gay sensuality that earlier painters gave to the devotees of Hymen.

Nevertheless, the picture was a great success in its time, and Reynolds himself was very much pleased with it. To Luke Gardiner he wrote: "The subject affords sufficient employment to the figures and gives an opportunity of introducing a variety of graceful historical attitudes."

Reynolds' plan was to progress from such classicized portraits to history pictures that did not pretend to be portraits at all. In this he was not successful. He did paint a few pure history pictures, such as the *Death of Dido,* almost embarrassing in its cloying classicism, but they won only moderate admiration, and he found little demand for them. It would be left to other painters, notably the American expatriate Benjamin West, to create a living school of history painting in Britain—one that would violate most of Reynolds' cherished principles.

While Reynolds was advancing step by step in his campaign to classicize British painting, Gainsborough was making fairly frequent visits to London from Bath. It was an arduous 105-mile journey, usually taking at least three days, although there were fast coaches called "flying machines" that started at 4 o'clock in the morning and made the trip with one brief overnight stop. Gainsborough probably traveled on horseback, which was much more comfortable than riding the springless coaches of the time, and went in the company of armed guards to be safe from the highwaymen who infested the road. It is likely that he broke his journey at Henley on the Thames, where his brother Humphry, the inventor, was the minister of a dissenting chapel and also manager of the locks on a canal.

Although Gainsborough had been one of the original members of the Royal Academy and was nominated to its governing council in 1775, he never bothered to attend an Academy meeting. Still, during his London visits, he must have heard a great deal about Reynolds' famous Discourses. If he did, they failed to influence him. Besides Van Dyck, he admired Murillo, Rembrandt and other old masters and sometimes took the trouble to copy their pictures for his own pleasure, but Reynolds' theories about ideal beauty and the vital importance to painting of classical poetry and history were not for him. His stock in trade was intuition combined with imagination, deft technical skill, an accurate eye, and a phenomenal memory for people, faces and things.

This did not mean that he was satisfied with what Reynolds called "cold" portraits, merely recording a likeness. He was wonderfully good at likenesses; he captured them quickly and with ease. But Gainsborough took little pleasure in this mechanical trick and wanted to do something more. Instead of trying to "rise," as Reynolds urged, to history paintings, he sought other escapes from competent but uninspired portraits. Landscapes, which expressed his abiding love of the country, were his lifelong favorite, and although he did not sell all that he painted, he did sell a good many, and even those he did not sell gave him deep pleasure.

Landscapes, however, were only one outlet. As Gainsborough grew in fame, skill and confidence, he developed ways to bring his poetic imagination to bear on portraiture. He still produced superlative likenesses; some of his sitters wanted nothing more. But when a spark of sympathy passed between him and the sitter, he often added a miraculous something that lit up the picture and still lights it up for present-day eyes.

The miracle often happened when he painted musicians, whom he regarded with warmth and admiration. His boldly posed portrait of Mrs. Thicknesse, a talented amateur musician, is rich in this more-than-likeness quality. So are his two portraits of Johann Christian Bach, son of the composer Johann Sebastian Bach, who was one of London's leading musicians and an intimate friend of Gainsborough's. Perhaps the most charming of his pictures of musicians is that of Lady Clarges, who combined qualities he admired. She was young, handsome and aristocratic-looking; she dressed in elaborate and beautiful clothes, and she was an accomplished harpist. So he painted her with poetry in his delighted brush. She is shown playing the harp, her fingers vaguely defined as if they were moving over the strings too quickly to be seen in detail. Her eyes are wide with pleasure, and she is smiling to herself as if enchanted with the music she is creating.

During his last years at Bath Gainsborough acquired an important patron in the Earl of Radnor, whose country seat was Longford Castle near Salisbury, about 40 miles from Bath. Perhaps because the earl was a genuine lover of painting, he seems to have been an exception to Gainsborough's rule of excluding noblemen as personal acquaintances. At Bath he had Gainsborough paint his portrait, a half-length for which he paid £63, and later he invited the artist to Longford to paint six members of his family.

The castle, built in Tudor times, is lived in today by the earl's descendants. It is an unusually charming place, even among England's famous country houses, facing a beautiful formal garden and surrounded by the kind of fertile rolling countryside that Gainsborough loved. The present Lord Radnor farms the castle's surrounding lands in a highly scientific manner, but he enjoys speculating about this ancestor's relationship with England's great portraitist. He points out that Gainsborough's established reputation and his membership in the Royal Academy would have made him an honored guest at Longford Castle. Instead of eating with the upper echelon of servants, as he might have done during his formative years in Ipswich, he probably had some of his meals in the informal breakfast room. He may not have seen the ladies of the house during the mornings, for they would have been drifting around in a state of dishabille, well covered but not presentable. Lord Radnor is sure, however, that Gainsborough took dinner with the family.

Five of the six portraits he painted are still at Longford Castle. They are simple head-and-shoulder lengths intended, probably at the earl's request, as family records, not for public exhibition. They show people who are as assured and happy as they are handsome. Painting them must have been a pleasure, for Gainsborough seems to have achieved more than just surface likenesses. The descendants of these people claim that they constantly see "Gainsborough faces" among their living relatives.

This happy assurance is missing, however, from one of the portraits Gainsborough did at Longford. When he started to paint Frances Duncombe, his penetrating intuition sensed another mood. She was an orphan of noble family, a connection of the Earl of Radnor's third wife, who was living at Longford and was engaged to marry the earl's eldest son. She was 16 and very pretty, but Gainsborough gave her a reserved, almost sad look. He painted her fullface; her eyes were on him, but they seemed to be looking somewhere else.

Unless she confided in him, which is not likely, he could not have known what troubled her, but some time after the picture was finished her secret was revealed when her fiancé intercepted an incriminating letter from a Mr. Arabin. Nothing was said until the occasion of a family dinner at the earl's London house on Grosvenor Street. Lord Radnor handed Frances the letter and asked: "What is the meaning of this; what have I or my son done to you that you should treat us in this manner, Miss Duncombe?" She fainted, was turned out of the house, and the engagement was broken off.

Miss Duncombe was not destitute, however, since she had estates of her own, and she seems to have lived a full though not a decorous life. She later married a Mr. Bowater, who was imprisoned for debt, and she is said to have been for a time "protected" by a German prince. Eventually she retired to her estate of Old Dalby Hall, Leicestershire, where she died at 69. Long before that, when she was 20, she had Gainsborough paint a second portrait, this one full length *(page 130)*. She is no longer the troubled young girl of Longford Castle but a stunningly beautiful young woman gorgeously dressed in the height of 18th Century finery. Perhaps she commissioned the portrait as a retort to Lord Radnor. Certainly no one could look less abashed or penitent.

In 1774, not long after painting his last portrait at Longford Castle, Gainsborough finally made his decision to move to London. There is a good deal of uncertainty about his reason. His friend Philip Thicknesse, putting himself as usual in the center of the action, claimed that a quarrel with him and his wife over an unfinished portrait led Tom to leave Bath so suddenly. Another suggestion is that Bath's market for expensive portraits had dried up; the artist Joseph Wright (generally called Wright of Derby), who moved to Bath shortly after Gainsborough left, found it impossible to make a living there. But Wright of Derby did not approach Gainsborough as a painter of aristocratic portraits. He was more an artist of the coming Industrial Revolution, so it is not surprising that he did not succeed in frivolous, fashionable Bath.

The truth about Gainsborough's move may be more complicated than these theories indicate. He had good informants in London artistic circles, and he could hardly help hearing that not all wealthy people who wanted their portraits painted by a superlative artist were pleased with the dogmas of Sir Joshua Reynolds. Some of the women certainly did not want to be shown with the features of Greek statues, sacrificing to an ancient god. Rich commissions were waiting in London for a painter willing to show women with human and personal, not "ideal," beauty.

Monument to Lordly Family

A bad case of gout was instrumental in bringing Gainsborough the patronage of the lord of one of England's most magnificent manors. Tormented by rheumatic joints, John, 4th Duke of Bedford often exchanged life at his ancestral estate of Woburn Abbey (*right*) for a season at Bath, where he eased his pain in the town's celebrated hot springs. He had been introduced to Gainsborough's work through two landscapes the artist had executed for him while still living in Ipswich. But in 1766 they became neighbors in the elegant circular row of houses in Bath known as the Circus, and proximity proved profitable to both. By the time the master of Woburn Abbey died five years later, Gainsborough had executed 14 paintings for him.

Many connoisseurs would have been content with such a treasure, but Woburn Abbey had miles of wall space to fill, and the fourth Duke's family insatiably acquired paintings, sculpture, and furnishings of many nations and eras. As the collection grew, several generations of architects added extensions to the Abbey that included such conceits as a Palladian greenhouse and a lakeside pavilion known as the Chinese Dairy.

Despite later alterations, much of Woburn Abbey survives as it was in Gainsborough's day, as the photographs on these pages show. The present Duke of Bedford welcomes the public, and visitors are dazzled by an opulence once viewed by only a privileged few.

Set in 3,000 acres of parkland 36 miles north of London, Woburn Abbey has been home to the Dukes of Bedford since about 1625. The estate derives its name from a medieval monastery that once stood on the site of the manor house.

Though the color has faded from the silk damask covering its walls, the Blue Drawing Room at Woburn Abbey has changed but little since the mid-1700s. Its harmonious juxtaposition of carved and gilded George II armchairs, French rococo furniture and the chaste pair of

Japanese vases over the door eloquently attests to a remarkably eclectic taste.

The first two paintings that the 4th Duke of Bedford bought in 1755 from Gainsborough are seen hanging in this room. A rustic scene, *Peasant with Two Horses*, is

110

displayed over the mantelpiece. To its right is a pastoral landscape that lends a romantic touch to the stately room, *Woodcutter Courting a Milkmaid (reproduced on page 96).*

The Duke, who combined a career of government service with the tireless pursuit of culture, attended to his correspondence at the ebonized writing table beneath his portrait by Gainsborough. To the right hangs a likeness of his daughter, Caroline, to the left one of his wife, Gertrude, and above the door a painting of her niece Mary—all of them by Gainsborough.

Woburn Abbey was overflowing with old masters and *objets d'art,* but there was always space for portraits. In addition to Gainsborough's works, those of his rival Sir Joshua Reynolds are also well represented. The family breakfast room *(opposite page)* is hung chiefly with paintings by Reynolds. The largest is his portrait of the fourth Duke's daughter-in-law, Lady Elizabeth Keppel, shown adorning an altar of love and clad in the bridesmaid's gown she wore at the wedding of King George III.

In the sumptuous State Dining Room *(above),* paintings of loftier personages seem more fitting than family likenesses. Here portraits in the grand manner by the Flemish master Van Dyck or a follower —including one of King Charles I—gazed down on the Abbey's most distinguished guests. The private dining room *(left),* where the family take their meals on less formal occasions, displays 21 views of Venice by the 18th Century Italian artist Canaletto. Both dining rooms glitter with a priceless array of silver and crystal.

A fascination with the exotic and the bizarre was widespread among British aristocrats, and inspired the Bedford who built Woburn Abbey to add the fantastic room known as The Grotto (above), its walls plastered with stucco dolphins and figures as well as thousands of real sea shells. Originally an open loggia, The Grotto was in time closed up, its arches blocked.

More than a century later the 4th Duke of Bedford indulged in his own imaginative flight and enhanced the Abbey with a Chinese chamber (right). It was decorated in Chinese Chippendale, a style of furniture combining a much-admired native English design with Oriental touches, but it contains exquisite authentic hand-painted wallpaper, shipped to England about 1750 on a voyage that took two years, and some rare porcelain pieces. One was meant to be filled with crickets; in such containers the little noisemakers traditionally served Chinese householders as a natural burglar alarm.

These touches stamped Gainsborough's ducal admirer as a man who dared to give his fancy free rein, and help explain the rapport that existed between patron and painter.

116

VI

Gainsborough's Challenge

When Gainsborough was 47 years old, he made his permanent move from Bath to London, riding the fine gray horse that his friend Wiltshire had given him. His wife and two daughters presumably traveled by stagecoach, with only a few household effects. Freight transport by wagon was expensive, and so when a family moved a considerable distance most heavy furniture was usually sold. In any case the new home in London would need a great deal of fresh furnishing, for it was part of a ducal mansion on Pall Mall, then one of the city's most fashionable streets.

Schomberg House, which would be Gainsborough's home from the early summer of 1774 until his death, was built about 1698 for the Duke of Schomberg, a German-born soldier who became the favorite general of King William III. It eventually came into the possession of John Astley, a painter who married a rich wife. Astley paid £5,000 for the stately mansion and spent an equal amount converting it into three large residences, each with its own entrance. Gainsborough rented the westernmost for £150 per year by one account, £300 by another. He may have made the choice partly because Astley, being a painter himself, was willing to let him fit his new home with a studio.

There were, of course, other reasons for selecting Schomberg House. One of them was prestige. Gainsborough had learned by experience at Bath that an impressive house at a fashionable address was almost essential for an ambitious portrait painter. The people who commissioned his pictures were themselves rich, and regarded visible signs of wealth as proof of worth. If he had chosen a modest residence he would have found it harder, if not impossible, to get established in London.

Another factor made Schomberg House an excellent choice for a painter who was about to challenge the redoubtable Sir Joshua Reynolds. A few yards away were the salesrooms of James Christie, London's leading auctioneer and picture dealer, whose firm is still active and famous today. Sooner or later everyone in London who was interested in painting came to Christie's and might be expected to stop in to see Gainsborough's pictures. This, too, was a lesson that he had learned in Bath, where his studio had benefited by being near the Abbey.

A pair of 21-year-old newlyweds, Squire William Hallett and his bride, Elizabeth, out for a morning stroll as soft breezes stir the greenery, personify the elusive charm of upper-class 18th Century England. Among Gainsborough's marriage paintings, this double portrait is perhaps the most beautiful.

The Morning Walk, c. 1785

In London Gainsborough needed all the strategies that he could muster, for conditions in the capital were far from favorable to him. Unlike Reynolds, who had made himself a leading social light, he had few backers in high society, so few that his friend Thicknesse was worried about the reception he would get. "I was much alarmed," he wrote in his biography of the artist, "lest with all his merit and genius, he might be in London a long time, before he was properly known to that class of people, who alone could *essentially* serve him, for of all the men I ever knew, he possessed least of that worldly knowledge, to enable him to make his own way into the notice of the GREAT WORLD. I therefore wrote to Lord Bateman who knew him, and who admired his talents . . . urging him at the same time for both our sakes, to give him countenance and make him known, that being all which was necessary."

Gainsborough moved into this mansion in a swank London neighborhood in 1774. The area was Pall Mall, named after the French croquetlike game *paille maille*, which was played there in the 17th Century. The residence was Schomberg House, named for the family that built it. Gainsborough's landlord, who was also an artist, had decorated the doorway with caryatids holding a relief of a female figure who symbolized painting. Gainsborough lived and worked behind this appropriate façade for 14 years, until his death.

Lack of influential friends was only one of Gainsborough's disadvantages. For several years after he arrived in London he remained on bad terms with the Royal Academy. Although he had been a member since the Academy's founding in 1768 and for a while had sent paintings to its exhibitions, he had attended no meetings and shown no interest in its affairs except its treatment of his own pictures. On this point Gainsborough was extremely touchy and unyielding. His first quarrel with the Academy had come in 1772 while he was still in Bath, and as a result he refused to send more paintings to its exhibitions until 1777. What brought about the dispute is uncertain, but a possible clue may be the following bit of gossip printed in London's *Public Advertiser* on May 4, 1772: "We hear, that the Gentlemen upon the Committee for managing the Royal Academy have been guilty of a scandalous meanness to a capital artist by secreting a whole length picture of an English Countess for fear their Majesties should see it; and this only upon a full conviction that it was the best finished picture sent this year to the exhibition. The same artist has been affronted in this manner several times before, from which they may depend upon his implacable resentment, and will hear from him in a manner that will very much displease them."

The affronted artist was Gainsborough, according to William Whitley, one of his biographers, and the portrait was probably of the widowed Lady Waldegrave, a nobleman's illegitimate daughter who had secretly married the Duke of Gloucester, the King's brother, much to the King's annoyance. Whitley's theory is that Reynolds, to avoid offending the Academy's royal patron, kept the portrait from being hung where the King would be sure to see it.

Gainsborough's temporary loss of the Academy as a place to show his pictures was such a serious handicap that it seems unlikely to have been brought about by a quarrel over a single picture. A more plausible conjecture is that he had become increasingly annoyed by the way all his pictures were displayed at the Academy. Indeed, its exhibitions were horrors by modern standards. Every inch of wall space in the large main hall was covered with pictures jammed together, frame to frame, often six rows deep. The lowest were so close to the floor that the viewer had to bend over to see them, and the topmost were almost out of sight under the high ceiling. A rigid rule declared that full-length portraits must be "on the line," which meant that their lower edges had to be level with the top of the doorways and nearly eight feet off the floor. If a visitor wanted to see them without serious distortion, he had to retreat halfway across the large room.

Artists quickly realized that if they wanted their pictures to attract attention at the Academy they must paint them with bold colors and firm outlines and not depend on fine touches that would be invisible half a room away. Many took to painting special "exhibition pictures" with the Academy in mind. Reynolds particularly made this adjustment. Only when a portrait of his was not to be shown in public did he use his more subtle techniques. If it was for exhibition, he made its colors so loud and strong that it would make an impact even on viewers craning their necks from far across the Academy's crowded floor. Many an artist compromised, first painting a picture for exhibition and later reworking it.

Gainsborough would do none of these things. Although he was influenced by contemporary taste he hated restraints that went contrary to his own judgment as to how he should paint. Therefore he continued to paint as if his pictures would be seen only in their final resting places, the walls of a town house or country mansion, where they would be hung at a proper height and viewed from the proper distance. Since the Academy did not always display pictures where they looked their best, he was often at odds with the hanging committee.

The same independent spirit that underlay his difficulties with the Academy characterized Gainsborough throughout his career. One notable expression of it was his refusal to paint "topographical" landscapes. A thriving market existed for views of country estates, but Gainsborough would not do them because he thought the artist, not nature, should control the composition of a picture. Long before he came to London he had aired his point of view in a letter to Lord Hardwicke, who apparently had requested a painting of his country home: "Mr. Gainsborough presents his Humble respects to Lord Hardwicke; and shall always think it an honour to be employ'd in anything for his Lordship; but with respect to *real Views* from Nature in this Country he has never seen any Place that affords a Subject equal to the poorest imitations of Gaspar or Claude [the French landscape painters Gaspard Poussin and Claude Lorraine]. Paul Sanby [Gainsborough's misspelling of Sandby, a British contemporary] is the only Man of Genius, he believes, who has employ'd his Pencil that way—Mr. G. hopes Lord Hardwicke will not mistake his meaning, but if his Lordship wishes to have anything tolerable of the name of G, the subject altogether . . . must be of his own Brain; otherwise Lord Hardwicke will only pay for Encouraging a Man out of his way and had much better buy a picture of some of the good Old Masters."

Independent though he was, Gainsborough could not, however, resist the almost universal desire of sitters to look better in their portraits than nature made them. But he never dodged the problem, as Reynolds often did, by idealizing the sitter. Instead he tried to make homely faces attractive while still resembling the originals and retaining their individuality. Usually he succeeded; most Gainsborough portraits are at least passably attractive but nearly all of them look alive and real.

The Georgian Style

These English home furnishings reflect the Georgian period's changing tastes. Below, fussy rococo carving *(top)* gave way to straightforward Neoclassic lines *(center)* around mid-century. A Greek Revival chair *(bottom)*, elegant if rather ponderous, was a result of the interest in antiquity. Opposite, increasing simplicity leads from an ornate candleholder through an embossed silver coffee set to pistol-grip flatware *(bottom)*.

Chippendale ribbon-back chair, c. 1754

Hepplewhite shield-back chair, c. 1786

Sheraton armchair, c. 1803

A striking exception to this rule is the second of two portraits that he painted of the Countess of Dartmouth. The first shows a formidable middle-aged woman decked out in pearls and ermine and holding a rose. She is stout and no beauty, but Gainsborough did all he could for her and at the same time tried to retain her character. This did not satisfy the earl, her husband, who wrote a series of letters asking for alterations. In his good-humored replies the artist blamed the portrait's lack of likeness (as the earl claimed) on the fancy 17th Century-style costume that the hefty countess had insisted on wearing. "I will venture to say," he wrote, "that had I painted Lady Dartmouth's Picture, dressed as her Ladyship goes, no fault . . . would have been found with it." He finally agreed to paint a new portrait if the countess would wear contemporary clothes. "My Lord," he wrote, "I am very well aware of the Objection to modern dresses in Pictures, that they are soon out of fashion & look awkward; but as that misfortune cannot be helped we must set it against the unluckiness of fancied dresses taking away Likenesses, the principal beauty and intention of a portrait." Not until his last letter did Gainsborough mention the earl's main objection to the original portrait. "All I mean is this," he promised, "Lady Dartmouth's Picture will look more like and not so large when dressed properly."

His second portrait of the countess shows her in a loose, informal robe and with the high hairdo fashionable at the time. She does not seem nearly as stout, which must have pleased her, but her vitality and forcefulness are gone. Her features are almost as characterless as the faces that Reynolds put on his classicized portraits. In complying with the earl's requests Gainsborough had yielded too much, and he knew by long experience that such yielding produces poor results.

Gainsborough must have liked Lord Dartmouth, for he was not always so accommodating. There are tales of portraits he refused to paint, and of others that went unfinished for years because he lost interest in them. Sometimes he stopped painting entirely to devote himself to playing the fiddle or learning to play other musical instruments that took his fancy, including the oboe and the harp. Even after he had become established in London he often put portraits aside for landscape painting or made trips to the countryside near the city or to Sudbury or Bath to renew his contact with the rural scenes that he loved so well.

When he did buckle down to commissions and admitted sitters to his London studio, they must have been surprised by his original methods. His "painting room" as he called it, was in itself unusual. Probably because he was largely self-taught, Gainsborough had never become attached to the notion, common among artists, that painting must be done in a steady north light. In Schomberg House the only rooms facing the north were at the front of the building and were much too small for a studio. He must have used one of the two large back rooms where the windows faced the south and on fine days admitted a glare of sunlight that more conventional artists would have found intolerable.

But light—or the lack of it—never bothered Gainsborough; he could and sometimes did paint in semidarkness. Especially when starting a portrait, he would close the shutters over the windows. The resulting dimness permitted him, he said, to block out the essentials of the picture without being distracted by details. Often he painted by candlelight, which is very dim indeed; a 25-watt bulb is about as bright as 21 candles.

Undoubtedly Gainsborough used stronger light to finish his portraits and get the colors right, but he kept in mind the conditions that they would meet in their permanent homes. The walls of 18th Century British mansions were seldom brightly lighted. In daytime the light came through comparatively small windows and often had to struggle past heavy curtains. Candles were the normal illumination after sundown.

Perhaps because they were painted to be viewed in subdued light, Gainsborough portraits show up much better in their intended homes than do those of other painters. Their pale faces and delicately colored draperies seem almost to glow in the dimness. This effect is not so striking in modern galleries, where the light can be controlled to suit any sort of picture, but in traditional private settings it is hard to miss. In Lord Radnor's art collection at Longford Castle, for example, the Gainsboroughs that have hung on the walls since they were painted two centuries ago far outshine Reynolds' portraits, whose generally ruddy tinge makes them look dark and smoky.

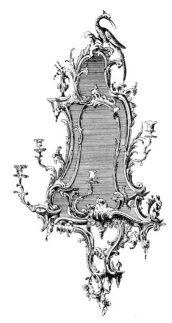

Girandole (candleholder), c. 1762

Besides his odd approach to lighting, Gainsborough used other unorthodox techniques that almost surely derived from his lack of formal training. Some of his brushes (he called them "pencils") had handles six feet long. When starting a portrait, he would place the sitter close to his easel. Then he would stand back and with his long brushes block out the likeness on the canvas. Apparently he found it useful to view both the real and the painted face from the same distance to ensure that they would appear to be the same size. Later, of course, he put down his long-handled brushes and finished the painting in a more conventional way.

Capturing a likeness was no difficulty for Gainsborough, and he did it with extraordinary speed. According to his biographer Thicknesse, he once painted a portrait of his nephew and apprentice Gainsborough Dupont in a single hour's sitting. Thicknesse tells a second story about Gainsborough's almost miraculous talent for likenesses, whatever the medium he used: "After returning from the Concert at Bath . . . where we had been charmed by Miss Linley's voice [Elizabeth Linley, a famous singer who later married the playwright Richard Sheridan], I went home to supper with my friend, who sent his servant for a bit of clay from the small beer barrel, with which he first modelled, and then coloured her head, and that too in a quarter of an hour, in such a manner that I protest it appeared to me even superior to his paintings! the next day I took a friend or two to his house to see it, but it was *not* to be seen, *the servant had thrown it down from the mantle piece and broke it.*"

Coffee service, 1799

Early in his career, Gainsborough developed a technique of giving the impression of roundness to a portrait's face by shading its cheeks and other curved surfaces with fine lines, somewhat like the crosshatching in an engraving. This method gave the picture a lively look, but not all his sitters liked it. When an Ipswich lawyer named Robert Edgar complained that the crosshatching was too noticeable in his portrait, Gainsborough wrote him a letter in his usual amiable tone. "You please me much," he

Georgian flatware

Opening day of the Royal Academy exhibit in 1787 found the usual crush of fashionable people jostling each other in the Great Room of Somerset House. In the center foreground of this engraving, the Academy's president, Sir Joshua Reynolds, ear trumpet in hand, stands next to the Prince of Wales and gestures toward his own portrait of a lady and three children, just to the right and above the open doorway. The congested atmosphere in the hall, its walls literally covered by canvases, repelled Gainsborough, who finally refused to show his pictures at the exhibits.

wrote, "by saying that no other fault is found in your picture than the roughness of the surface, for that part being of use in giving force to the effect at a proper distance, and what a judge of painting knows an original from a copy by; in short being the touch of the pencil, which is harder to preserve than smoothness. I am much better pleas'd that they should spy out things of that kind, than to see an eye half an inch out of its place, or a nose out of drawing when viewed from a proper distance. I don't think it would be more ridiculous for a person to put his nose close to the canvas and say the colours smell offensive, than to say how rough the paint lies; for one is just as material as the other with regard to hurting the effect and drawing of a picture."

Gainsborough was explaining a principle that artists have discovered and rediscovered many times: fine brushwork can look coarse or even ugly when examined too closely, but from a distance of several feet, the brushstrokes merge and create the illusion of smoothness. Gainsborough eventually abandoned hatching, however. It was against contemporary taste, which wanted the brushwork of a portrait to remain smooth even when viewed from a few inches away. Most of the portraits that he painted in Bath and London have this fine-grained finish.

For painting landscapes Gainsborough developed other unusual techniques. As he pointed out to Lord Hardwicke, a landscape to him was not the picture of an existing place; it was a composition built out of elements that he had seen and stored in his memory or sketchbook. When planning such a work he made preliminary drawings, as he sometimes did for portraits, and to help the process of composition he brought into his studio a collection of oddments such as branches, weeds, rocks and even live animals, including pigs and donkeys. In Whitley's biography of Gainsborough appears an account by an unidentified "Amateur of Painting" telling how the artist put these things to use: "I had the honor to be acquainted with that truly British genius at Bath, and have more than once sat by him of an evening and seen him make models—or rather thoughts—for landscape scenery on a little old-fashioned folding oak table. . . . This table, held sacred for the purpose, he would order to be brought to his parlor, and thereon compose his designs. He would place cork or coal for his foregrounds; make middle grounds of sand and clay, bushes of moss and lichens, and set up distant woods of broccoli."

The bushes of moss and the broccoli forests served Gainsborough as an easily rearranged framework to assist him in visualizing a scene which his vivid invention then clothed with detailed but poetic reality and peopled with carefully drawn human figures. His earlier landscapes show more details than the eye can see without close examination, but later he turned to a less painstaking style, making a few strokes of the brush suggest a rock or a branch of green leaves. His use of this technique predated the French Impressionists by nearly a century.

Some landscapes painted after Gainsborough moved to London show a remarkable combination of coarse and fine brushwork. Such a one is his well-known scene *The Market Cart*. Gainsborough finished most of the picture, especially its animals and human figures, with smooth, delicate strokes like those in his later portraits. Then he apparently stood back with a brush charged with white paint (perhaps one of his long-handled brushes) and quickly applied white highlights. A girl's cap, a dog, the forehead of a horse all got their final dabs of white, most of which are much less refined than the underlying brushstrokes. These white flecks light up *The Market Cart* and give it vigorous life.

Even more astonishing is the effect gained by a few, deft brushstrokes in a Gainsborough landscape now in the National Gallery in Washington. Three peasants, one of whom is riding a horse, are seen crossing a bridge. The man walking behind the horse is composed of only nine strokes done with a broad, rather dry brush; the horse, its rider and the man walking alongside are made up of about 40 strokes all together. A dog walking ahead of the group consists of only three brushstrokes.

When looked at closely, the figures in *Mountain Landscape with Bridge* *(page 181)* dissolve into meaningless streaks and scratches. But as the viewer moves back from the picture and the eye fills in the framework provided by the sparse but skillful brushstrokes, the figures clothe themselves miraculously in abundant detail. At a distance of 10 or 15 feet the peasants, their horse and their dog become full, round, moving figures. They even reflect a mood; they are weary, returning home from the day's work.

Such experimentation with the extraordinary tricks that brushes and paint can play on the suggestible human eye increased as Gainsborough grew older. After he settled in London in 1774 he became more experimental than at any other time of his career, and his success in the great city owed much to his mastery of unusual techniques. Despite his difficulties with the Royal Academy, the year after he moved to London he was able to write to his sister Mrs. Gibbon, the lodginghouse keeper at Bath: "What will become of me time must show; I can only say that my present situation with regard to encouragement is all that heart can wish."

I'm sick of portraits," Gainsborough exploded one day. Often he dreamed of abandoning his lucrative trade among the sophisticates of Bath and London and of returning to the simple country life of his boyhood —wandering in the woods and sketching landscapes.

Far from abandoning portraits, Gainsborough actually produced more than 700 of them—"To make the pot boil" was his explanation. But for all his cynicism about portraiture, he worked tremendously hard at the art, sometimes taking more than a year on a canvas. This was hardly potboiling. When we look at these portraits we are struck by the care he took in getting the folds of a satin gown exactly right, and we can sense the special pleasure he took in painting sitters for whom he felt a strong affinity.

Gainsborough's portraits are a gallery of an extraordinary group of people. He captured on his canvases not only the look but the very spirit of Britain's aristocrats, soldiers, squires, statesmen, and assorted folk of leisure and means. They lived with style in both city and countryside. They relished the theater, politics and gossip. They were supreme optimists, the leading citizens of the most vigorous nation in the world. And, if they were also a bit smug, at least they tolerated among themselves a delightful assortment of eccentricities. With his portraits, Gainsborough immortalized the fascinating face of 18th Century England.

Fair Faces of England

In his painting of Lady Sheffield *(right, and page 137)*, with her soft hair and glowing skin under a beribboned hat, Gainsborough typified the look of the woman of fashion of his day.

Lady Sophia Charlotte Sheffield, 1785-1786, detail

William Wollaston, late 1750s

Gainsborough sought out people who shared his love for music, and when they sat for him he usually painted them with their instruments. William Wollaston, who later represented Ipswich in Parliament, agreed to forgo a formal pose in favor of this relaxed view with his flute and sheet music. It is possible that he, Anne Thicknesse (right) and Gainsborough played chamber music together; in any case, the enthusiasm the three shared animates both portraits.

126

Mrs. Philip Thicknesse, 1760

Anne Ford was the wife of Philip Thicknesse, Gainsborough's social mentor at Ipswich and Bath. She was a gifted musician who dabbled in belles-lettres and could chat in five languages. Her pose—cradling a guitar, her viola da gamba nearby—was considered provocatively casual by her contemporaries, but she loved the painting and never sold it. In her 87th year, it was noted that "her eyesight was as perfect as at twenty" and she still had her teeth.

William Poyntz, c. 1762

Another sitter Gainsborough posed informally was William
Poyntz, whose social credentials were lofty (brother of a
countess) but recent (grandson of an upholsterer). The
128   portrait brought Gainsborough his first London press notice,

which admired the dog as well as his owner. This must have
pleased Poyntz, for shortly before the portrait was painted the
spaniel, Amber, had routed a burglar from under his
master's bed, and Poyntz wished such fidelity memorialized.

Captain Wade, 1771

William Wade, master of ceremonies and social arbiter of the resort of Bath, demanded that Gainsborough portray him in the most elegant, formal and flattering manner possible, the better to impress elite visitors to the spa. Soon after the painting was hung at Bath, an anonymous wag pronounced this judgment: "All at once I was struck with the portrait of Wade, / Which, tho' like him in features, is much too tall made / And looks, like its Master—ashamed of his trade."

The Honorable Frances Duncombe, 1777-1778

130

Gainsborough painted the flirtatious, décolleté Frances Duncombe two years after a compromising note from an admirer had caused the severance of her engagement to a viscount and her expulsion from his family's home. Left to fend for herself, Frances made the most of her attractions, and besides marrying an Englishman she is said to have been the mistress of a German prince. After her death, her effects were put up for auction; this portrait went for seven pounds.

The Honorable Mrs. Graham, 1775–1777

Mary Graham posed for Gainsborough about a year after she married a wealthy Scotsman. The play of light on rich textures (detail next page) lends the portrait a romantic quality. After 18 years of blissful marriage Mary fell ill and died while traveling in the South of France. On the journey home, her casket was broken open by a drunken mob of revolutionaries and her body was exposed. Thereafter, her husband could never bear to look at the painting.

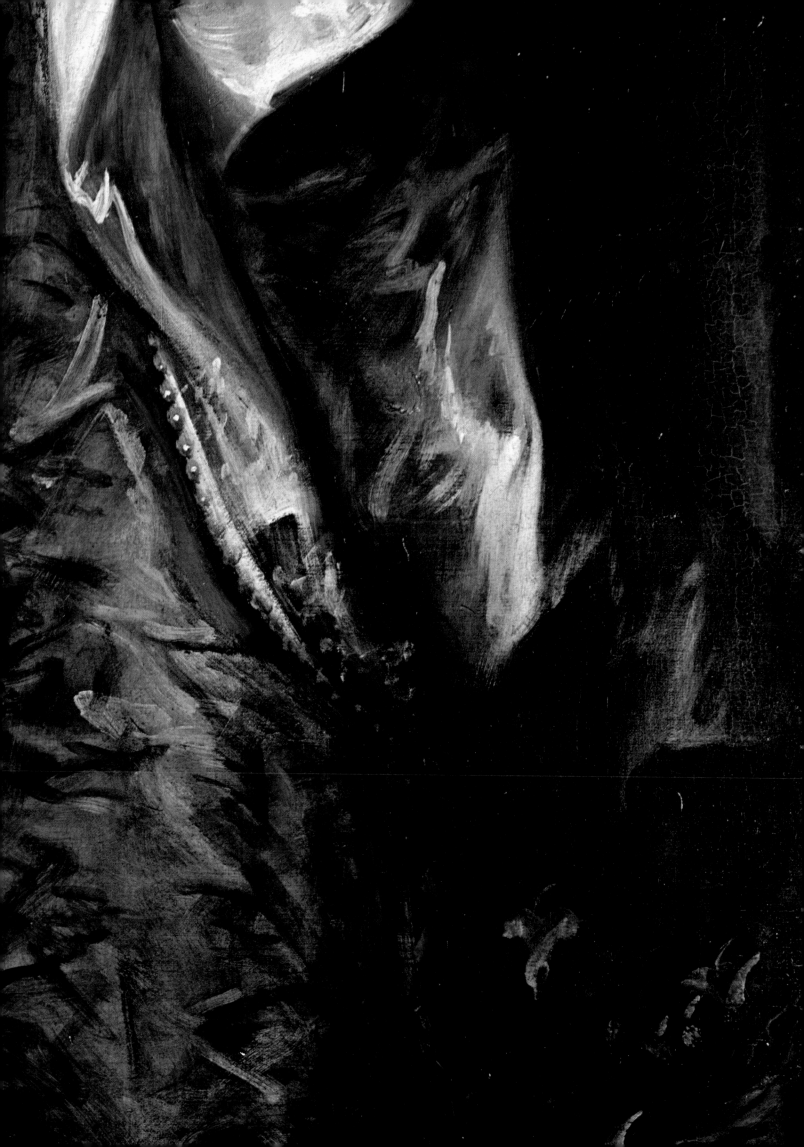

Mrs. Grace Dalrymple Elliott, exhibited 1778

"*If to her share some female errors fall / Look on her face and you'll forget them all.*" *Summing up the attitude of an age indulgent to beauty, these lines by the poet Alexander Pope were offered in the London "General Evening Post" to describe Gainsborough's portrait of Grace Dalrymple Elliott. A divorcee, she enjoyed such notoriety as a demimondaine that the Prince of Wales and a Lord Cholmondeley vied for the distinction of being declared father of her bastard child.*

Mrs. "Perdita" Robinson, 1781-1782

The actress Mary Robinson was popularly known as Perdita because while playing that role in "The Winter's Tale" she became the mistress of the Prince of Wales. Gainsborough painted her holding a miniature of her royal lover. When the Prince's ardor cooled she turned to other men; later, she became a writer. Her parties attracted the cream of society, but she was chronically in debt. Her Gainsborough portrait was sold and in time was acquired by the Prince.

Mrs. Siddons, c. 1783-1785

Sarah Siddons, the leading tragedienne of the Drury Lane Theatre, was painted by both Reynolds and Gainsborough. When she first posed for Reynolds he said: "Ascend your undisputed throne and graciously bestow upon me some good idea of the tragic muse." He then proceeded to paint her in his classical grand manner. Gainsborough, on the other hand, portrayed her in simple street dress. As for flattery the best he could manage was "Damn the nose, there's no end to it."

136

Lady Sophia Charlotte Sheffield, c. 1785

One of the last of Gainsborough's portraits was that of Lady Sophia Charlotte Sheffield. Her husband's family, founded by the illegitimate son of a duke, was now firmly established in the aristocracy, and she presided over a large estate in Lincolnshire in the manner prescribed by the Sheffield motto —"Politely, but firmly." She was in her early twenties when Gainsborough painted her, but her mature expression reflects the responsibility—and security—of her position.

Mrs. Richard Brinsley Sheridan, probably exhibited 1783

Described by an admiring bishop as "the connecting link between woman and angel," Elizabeth Ann Linley was the daughter of a music teacher at Bath. Gainsborough, who knew her as a child, was one of many who loved to hear her sing. She is said to have given her first recital at the age of 12, and at 19 she was performing before the King and fashionable audiences. Her beauty attracted many men, whose advances she rebuffed, but in 1772 she eloped with the playwright Richard Brinsley Sheridan. She forswore nearly all public appearances to look after the accounts of the Drury Lane Theatre, managed by her husband, and she shared his devotion to politics, campaigning actively for the Whig Party. Gainsborough depicted her as serious but also relaxed, as if she had just pulled off her hat and plopped down under a tree in the countryside.

VII

London
Triumph

Gainsborough's biographers do not shed much light on his first few years in London. Only a few of his paintings are known to date from between 1774 and 1777, and some writers have taken this to mean that he had trouble getting started in the capital. On the other hand he seldom dated or even signed his pictures, and during the period when he was at odds with the Royal Academy none were entered in its records. So he could have painted many unlisted pictures, and very likely he did. Certainly he showed no sign of economic stress. He was able to maintain his expensive residence at Schomberg House, and by 1777 he had his own carriage as well as a footman, both costly acquisitions.

For a while, however, the novelty of living in the great, exciting capital may have diverted Gainsborough from the pursuit of commissions. He spent a lot of time with his musical and theatrical friends and experimenting with new painting techniques. At the Drury Lane Theatre he became fascinated by the dramatic effects that the scene designer Philippe de Loutherbourg achieved using transparent paints, which he had recently introduced. Stage scenery and pictures done in these paints could be lighted from behind, and when the composers Carl Friedrich Abel and Johann Christian Bach were decorating a concert room, Gainsborough was one of the artists who contributed large paintings in the new medium. The glow from banks of candles shining through the pictures not only produced a striking effect but illuminated the entire room. No trace survives of these unusual paintings; they were probably treated as theatrical scenery and discarded when they were soiled or damaged.

Gainsborough's period of ease in London, if such it was, did not last long. In 1777, after a good deal of negotiation as to how his pictures would be hung, he made peace with the Royal Academy and that year sent to its exhibition a sensational group of portraits. The two that attracted the most attention were of the Duke and Duchess of Cumberland. The Duchess was a very beautiful woman; Gainsborough did her full justice and gave her a flirtatious, lighthearted look for which she was probably grateful because it belied the fact of her married life. The Duke, a brother of King George's, was not only dull but notoriously unfaithful. Several

The eminent actor David Garrick was painted by his friend Gainsborough no less than five times, but this portrait, showing him nonchalantly leaning against a bust of Shakespeare, best captured the winning essence of this vain but immensely talented man. Mrs. Garrick thought so, pronouncing it the best of all the many portraits ever painted of her husband. Gainsborough was attracted to theatrical personalities and he was especially fond of Garrick, whom he once described as "the greatest living creature in every respect."

years before Gainsborough painted him, England had rung with the scandal of his open affair with Lady Grosvenor, for which he was forced to pay £10,000 in damages to Sir Richard Grosvenor, the lady's husband. Gainsborough's sympathy was obviously with the Duchess, for he gave the Duke of Cumberland a sly, untrustworthy expression that must have delighted gossips. It is a wonder that the Duke accepted his almost libelous portrait; perhaps he was too stupid to realize how unpleasant he had been made to look. This was not the only time that Gainsborough expressed his aversion to a sitter in a painting. In the Corcoran Museum in Washington are full-length portraits of Lord and Lady Dunstanville that make clear how he felt about the couple. Milord appears as an overdressed dolt while milady sparkles with mischievous beauty.

Also in the Royal Academy's exhibition of 1777 was the superb full-length painting of Mrs. Thomas Graham *(page 131)*, now in the National Galleries of Scotland. She was not yet 20 when Gainsborough painted her, but was already a famous beauty. He obviously enjoyed the job of portraying this dazzling creature; he painted all her finery—silks, pearls, ostrich feathers—down to the last gleaming detail. The petulant look that he gave her adds to the picture's haughty effect and no doubt contributed to its triumphant reception by London's aristocrats.

After his success at the 1777 exhibition Gainsborough was in great demand, and from then to the end of his life he had all the portrait business he wanted or could handle. Some of his sitters he painted rather indifferently, but when he saw in one of them something that aroused his creative imagination his brushes worked wonders. Women were never more beautiful, men never more handsome than when Gainsborough at the peak of his powers gave them his full poetic attention. By 1780 he had been summoned to the court to do portraits of the Royal Family, and when he painted Queen Charlotte he made her as regal and attractive as any queen ever portrayed.

How he got his first commissions to paint the Royal Family is not definitely known; it may have been partly due to the fact that Sir Joshua Reynolds was not popular at court. Reynolds' eminence as an artist had won him the presidency of the Royal Academy and the King had knighted him, but because of his association with Whig Party leaders bent on curbing royal power, George III was less than cordial to him. This made Gainsborough the next in line for royal favor. Except when painting Queen Charlotte, however, he does not seem to have enjoyed his work at the palace. George III was already showing signs of the insanity that clouded his later years, and few of his relatives were either handsome or interesting. Some of Gainsborough's portraits of these lofty personages are perfunctory, indicating that his enthusiasm was at a low ebb.

Royal favor was important to Gainsborough, but even before he painted at the court, other sources had made him famous. At all literate levels of 18th Century British society, painting and painters were more widely discussed than they are now. Art exhibitions were jammed with visitors even when high admission was charged. The press ran numerous criticisms of painters' works, and gossipy journalists publicized their sales and sitters. For people who read newspapers, painters were news.

A good deal of credit for Gainsborough's celebrity belongs to a parson-turned-newspaper-editor, the Reverend Henry Bate, who became his staunch friend and highly partisan champion. Even for the 18th Century, when colorful behavior was almost expected of men in the public eye, Bate was exceptional. He had taken holy orders after studying at Oxford but preferred hunting and athletic contests to clerical duties. In 1772 he helped found the London *Morning Post* and conducted it in such a lively, often libelous manner that he was continually embroiled in battles with prominent persons whom he fought in print to the delight of his large readership. When he founded the *Morning Herald* in 1780, he conducted it in the same vigorous way.

Some of Bate's personal exploits were as spectacular as the battles he waged in his papers. Although a clergyman, he loved the theater and delighted in the company of young actresses. Just before Gainsborough came to London in 1744, Bate took one of his actress friends, a Mrs. Hartley, to Vauxhall, the city's smart amusement center. His companion was well known for her beauty and figure (David Garrick, the famous actor, had said "her make is perfect"), and a gang of fashionable bullies started to admire her offensively. So that no one would spoil their sport they had brought along a bodyguard, a professional prize fighter disguised in gentlemen's clothes. But the Reverend Bate was a fighter himself; with his fists he thrashed the bodyguard and scattered Mrs. Hartley's molesters. The episode caused a sensation, the *Morning Post* made the most of it and it helped to earn Bate the nickname of "The Fighting Parson."

It was this formidable man who made it his business to praise and promote his artist friend on every occasion. Other newspaper critics admired the pictures that Gainsborough sent to the Academy exhibition in 1777, and compared him cautiously with the reigning Reynolds. But Bate made no bones about it. His *Morning Post* proclaimed: "As the pencil of this gentleman has evidently entitled him to this distinction we have impartially placed him at the head of the artists we are about to review." The paper went on to praise in extravagant terms every Gainsborough in the show. It left no doubt that as far as the *Morning Post* was concerned Gainsborough was a better painter than Reynolds.

The stridency of the *Morning Post* and the counterstridency of newspapers championing Sir Joshua probably account for the widespread idea that Gainsborough and Reynolds were bitter personal enemies. It is true that they were rivals in the sense that they were competitors in the limited market for expensive, fashionable portraits, but neither man was bitter or quarrelsome by nature. Each was fully conscious of the talents of the other. Gainsborough was once heard to exclaim, while admiring Reynolds' works: "Damn him! How various he is!" and Reynolds was sufficiently appreciative of Gainsborough to buy one of his pictures, the *Girl with Pigs*. Shortly after he did so, Gainsborough offered to paint Reynolds' portrait, but the sittings were broken off when Sir Joshua became ill; they were never resumed, perhaps because Reynolds did not offer to paint Gainsborough's portrait in return. This was the nearest approach to a quarrel between the two men.

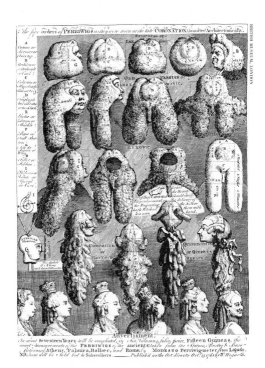

In the engraving above, Hogarth poked fun at the extravagant wigs of the *haut monde*: he divided the hairpieces into five groups, akin to classical architectural orders, and labeled and measured them with a precision meant to mock the pedantry of the archeologists busy classifying artifacts in Greece. Another parody of chic hairdos *(below)* proposed an extensible carriage body to enable a lady to go out via a tall second-story window with headdress intact.

Nevertheless, Reynolds was deeply affected by the great success in London of those portraits by Gainsborough that captured not only a sitter's likeness but his personality as well. Although he continued to paint his classicized portraits with "ideal," characterless faces, Reynolds also began to paint portraits that had more life and individuality, even traces of humor. For a while he still insisted on dressing his women patrons in flowing robes, but he no longer depicted them with the sterile sexlessness of his pseudo-Greek muses. When he painted the Countess of Harrington he made her an exciting, even dangerous woman, with hot eyes, a sensual mouth and pointed ears. Joanna Leigh, an actress, he portrayed carving her lover's initials in the bark of a tree. He made her a real and living woman, and the hitherto discreet Sir Joshua even permitted the feminine curves of her body to show provocatively through the folds of her robe. This titillating picture was exhibited at the Royal Academy in 1776, and one can imagine Gainsborough, a lifelong connoisseur of pretty girls, standing before it and smiling his approval.

Gainsborough was not influenced in turn by Sir Joshua or by anyone else. He persisted in ignoring the classical lore from which most painters of the time drew inspiration. People were his inspiration, and a wonderful assortment of them passed through his London painting room. There were the usual elegantly dressed dukes and duchesses, earls and countesses, as well as lesser members of the landed aristocracy, and since he loved the theater he also painted many of its stars, particularly actresses. Most of these fascinating, long-limbed beauties were also famous demimondaines, sometimes called "cruisers on the Cyprian coast," a phrase of the day referring to the birth of Venus from the sea off the island of Cyprus. Among the most notorious was Giovanna Baccelli, an Italian dancer, who distinguished herself by accompanying the British Ambassador, the Duke of Dorset, to France, and appearing on the Paris stage wearing the ribbon of his Order of the Garter. Gainsborough's portrait of her makes her look worthy of the devotion of a Duke-Ambassador.

An even more successful "cruiser" was the stately Mrs. Elliott *(page 134)*, popularly known as Dolly the Tall. In his *Morning Herald* the Reverend Bate described her jewels as having "a splendor that might almost rival that of the Emperor of the East, for each hand aches with the treasure it carries." Gainsborough did her justice also, but the lady of Cyprus whom he made most appealing was Mrs. Robinson *(page 135)*, nicknamed "Perdita" from a part she played in a production of Shakespeare's *The Winter's Tale*.

When Gainsborough painted Perdita in 1782, she had recently broken off a widely publicized affair with the Prince of Wales, and gossip said that she refrained from publishing his love letters only after he had paid her £10,000—the same amount that his uncle, the Duke of Cumberland, had paid to Sir Richard Grosvenor for damages to his lady. Other rich and noble admirers soon besieged her, but Gainsborough did not make her look like a mercenary courtesan. His extraordinary feeling for character told him that she was more than that. Her portrait, one of his most famous pictures, reveals her as not only beautiful but also notably intelligent and hints that in spite of her lurid reputation, she could be capable of selfless devotion. In this conjecture the artist was right. Not long after her portrait was painted, Perdita fell in love with the dashing Colonel Banastre Tarleton, who had led British troops in the colonies during the American War of Independence. He was neither rich nor noble, but for him she deserted her wealthy and highborn suitors. When Tarleton, hounded by debt, was about to flee the country, she tried to intercept him with money to pay his creditors. In the coach headed for a British port she was nearly frozen to death and was permanently paralyzed. Not at all daunted, she undertook a new profession and became a successful writer of plays, poetry, and magazine and newspaper articles.

The glamor of Gainsborough's sitters suggests that even at the peak of his fame in London he led an active social life, but in all probability this was not the case. If it had been, he would have been mentioned more frequently by the numerous memoir, letter and gossip writers of the time, who recorded any notables they saw at fashionable dinners and balls. Neither did he entertain at Schomberg House, for his home life was far from agreeable. An undated letter to his sister, Mrs. Gibbon, who kept the lodginghouse in Bath, tells of his artistic success but complains about his wife's obsession with money. "I was induced," he wrote, "to try . . . giving into her Hands every Farthing of the Money as I earned it, but very soon found that . . . it was a further incouragement to Govern me, and invert the order of Nature in making the Head the foot and the foot the Head; so that now I have taken the staff into my own hands again, and purpose (God willing) to try my own Virtue and strength to walk straight and do the best for my Children let them follow the Vanity of the Age, or the weakness of their leader as they will."

The best he could do for his two daughters, who had been such appealing little girls and had grown into handsome young women, was not enough to give them happy homes of their own. Perhaps the mental confusion that was to afflict their later years was already showing, for in spite of their good looks and their father's prosperity and fame, they seem to have had no suitors except an eccentric oboe player named Johann Christian Fischer, who surreptitiously courted both. Gainsborough admired his oboe playing, but did not think he would make a good husband. He was right in this judgment, for soon after Fischer married the artist's daughter Mary in 1780, the pair separated, and Mary was back at Schomberg House. Margaret never married, and both daughters became increasingly strange as they grew older.

Since Gainsborough's home life was so unsatisfactory, it is not surprising that he sought diversion elsewhere. There is no evidence that he kept a mistress, though such relationships were common at the time and not much decried. But his interest in the theater and the numerous portraits he painted of ladies of Cyprus imply that he did not lack the company of attractive and compliant women.

He also did a good deal of drinking. After his death, a correspondent of the *Monthly Mirror* claimed that Gainsborough had once gone to a party at the home of a musical friend where he drank so much that he fell in the street on his way home and could not get up. A "woman of the town" found him sleeping like a log, put him in a coach and took

Wealthy young men who toured Europe often acquired a passion for things Italian and became known as "Macaronis." Even the botanist Joseph Banks, whose scientific pursuits baffled his society friends, could not escape a ribbing as "The Fly Catching Macaroni." Later Macaronis, called Dandies, showed less enthusiasm for study than for clothes; they developed an outlandish costume *(below)*, its wasp-waist effect heightened by stuffing a pillow under the shirt to achieve a pouter-pigeon bosom.

As literacy spread in 18th Century England, professional writers achieved public notice before artists. Caricaturists had a field day satirizing the literary men. When Alexander Pope attacked his critics in a poem, "The Dunciad," they replied with this engraving *(above)* of Pope as a monkey-pope with an ass for a prime minister. To help raise the status of authors, Samuel Johnson wrote biographies of famous poets, only to be caricatured *(below)* as a shortsighted owl who had failed to see his subjects clearly.

him to her lodgings. When he woke up alone next morning he did not know where he was and soon discovered that his watch and his pocketbook, which contained the considerable sum of £430, were gone. The woman shortly appeared. As the *Monthly Mirror* described it: "She then told him that the book and watch were in her possession, and informed him of the manner in which she had discovered him, and the following circumstances. It was her misfortune, she told him, to be connected with a young man of bad habits and disposition, who, had he visited her on the previous night, as she expected, would have robbed him of everything valuable. Gainsborough gave her the odd £30, and having thanked her, departed. He continued a friend to her till her death."

Another story of Gainsborough's sometimes erratic behavior is told by his biographer Whitley. Once when the artist was dining with David Garrick he met Reynolds' literary mentor, Dr. Samuel Johnson. "But unfortunately through watching Johnson," says Whitley, "the painter, himself a sensitive and impressionable man, acquired some of his habits of involuntary twitching and gesticulation. For a month or two Gainsborough could not keep still, sleeping or waking. 'In fact,' said he, 'I became as full of megrims as the old literary leviathan himself, and fancied that I was changed into a Chinese automaton, and condemned incessantly to shake my head.'"

This strange conduct may have been a joke at the expense of Dr. Johnson and his solemn circle, for Gainsborough hated discussions he considered weighty or dull. There is no evidence that he paid attention to politics or other public matters. When he arrived in London in 1774, Britain was on the brink of the American War of Independence, which tried her sorely and resulted in her first telling defeat in several centuries. Except for remarking in a letter that his footman, David, dared not go out on the street for fear of being pressed into the Navy, Gainsborough left no indication that he was conscious of the war, though some of its outstanding military figures passed through his painting room. Besides Colonel Tarleton, the debt-ridden lover of Perdita Robinson, he painted General Thomas Gage, who commanded British troops during the Battles of Lexington and Bunker Hill, and General Charles Cornwallis, who surrendered to George Washington at Yorktown.

Gainsborough was equally unconcerned with the Industrial Revolution, which was proceeding all around him. By the last quarter of the 18th Century, British science and technology were already far ahead of the rest of the world, and ghastly industrial "black towns" with chimneys belching coal smoke would soon spread over England's north and Midlands. But no hint of this portentous development appeared in Gainsborough's work. Most other artists of the time also ignored it. About the only one who realized that a new age was coming to Britain and the world was Joseph Wright of Derby, who failed to make a living as a portrait painter in Bath. He was fascinated by science and technology, and some of his paintings are dramatic studies of scientific experiments, of forges and textile mills, of the play of light on machinery.

Such things as factories had no appeal for Gainsborough. Doubtless he considered them ugly and repellent. Although he never identified himself with the lords and ladies whom he painted so gloriously, he was closely associated with their enchanted world where all was pomp and silk and glitter. The war in America meant little to The Great World of London. The aristocrats who dominated society drew their wealth from land, not from foreign trade, which was hurt worst by the war. They still had plenty of money for Gainsborough's portraits, apparently more than ever, and his landscapes were selling also, to his delight. Britain's defeat and the loss of the 13 American colonies had not the slightest effect on his fortune or spirits. He continued to paint the portraits of wealthy aristocrats, sometimes recording their faces and characters with almost cruel clairvoyance and sometimes, when the mood was on him, making them look as lofty and attractive as they yearned to be. His portrait of Mr. and Mrs. William Hallett, *The Morning Walk (page 116)*, now in the National Gallery, London, is the peak of this artificial but charming style. It has been justly called "the spirit of the 18th Century."

How to harrow up the Soul — Oh — h — h !

Bᵁᵀ there was another side to Gainsborough that rebelled against The Great World of London. In spite of his prosperity and the life he led in the capital, surrounded by the people and symbols of high society, he remained a countryman at heart and yearned to retire to the country. To his fellow music lover William Jackson he had written: "I'm sick of Portraits and wish very much to take my Viol da Gamba and walk off to some sweet Village when I can paint Landskips and enjoy the fag End of Life in quietness and ease." The nearest he got to this ideal was to take a house at Richmond, which is now a suburb of London but was then fairly rural. In this retreat he spent his summers, but it was not sufficiently far away for total seclusion. Sometimes even the King, who spent much time at his residence in nearby Kew, came to call on him there.

Celebrities in all walks of life were fair game for satirists. The success of the actress Sarah Siddons provoked an envy that found outlet in the engraving above, accusing her of ham acting. Actually, Mrs. Siddons cultivated a stately stage presence to intimidate the raucous playgoers of the age. Another well-known figure, the Archbishop of Canterbury *(right, below)*, was chided for nepotism: his donkey has the face of his son-in-law, who was also Dean of Canterbury.

Gainsborough's real escape from the artificial world of high society was through his mind and his painting, especially in a development that began during his later years in London. He had almost always put people in his landscapes, but during most of his life he regarded them as secondary. In his correspondence with William Jackson he once described them as something to "fill a place . . . or to create a little business for the Eye to be drawn from the Trees in order to return to them with more glee." Furthermore, these human figures were generally small and represented idealized peasants, well fed and well dressed, or carefree gypsies gathered sociably around their campfire. In using such people as decorations in his paintings, Gainsborough seldom made it apparent that he had any knowledge of their often desperate poverty in real life, or that he sympathized with them.

An ASS loaded wᵗʰ PREFERMENTS.

The knowledge and sympathy were there, however, deep in his heart, and they eventually showed in his painting. Around 1780 he began to produce an entirely different kind of landscape with people. The human figures were no longer mere decorations. Sometimes they occupied a large part of the canvas, and even when they were small, they dominated its mood. Their faces were sad; their clothes were rags, and they lived in cottages no better than hovels. These pictures expressed a touching concern for the poor and the humble, and they proved that Gainsborough, the painter of aristocracy, never lost touch with the less favored world.

A Good Time to be Alive

Despite the class distinctions of 18th Century England, the lofty and the humble made common cause in the vigorous pursuit of pleasure. Possibilities for enjoyment abounded. Restless gentlemen and members of the rising middle class found it in tours of the countryside or in the delights of the horse; wealthy landowners mingled with shopkeepers and simple rustics to revel in the lusty gaiety of local fairs. Londoners had their own pet diversions: the fashionable and the masses alike crowded so-called pleasure gardens, such as Ranelagh and Vauxhall (also known as Spring Gardens), whose leafy promenades proved a perfect place for the breeding of scandal and the exchange of gossip. The literary arbiter of the age, the pompous Dr. Samuel Johnson, dined often at Vauxhall, while even the most self-inflated member of the Royal Family, the Duke of Cumberland *(right)*, deigned to favor the people with occasional forays into their midst.

Among the talented artists who, in the second half of the century, recorded their countrymen in moments of relaxation were George Stubbs and Thomas Rowlandson. Stubbs, because of his extraordinary passion for animals, became the inevitable favorite of the horsy set. Rowlandson's great gifts with pen and watercolor served as a springboard for social commentary as perceptive and biting as Hogarth's. Rowlandson saw his world both buttoned and unbuttoned, and left a matchless pictorial chronicle of the English at ease.

The embodiment of arrogance —booted and spurred, peering haughtily through an oversized opera glass—the Duke of Cumberland, one of the younger brothers of the Prince of Wales, strides into a public building in this Rowlandson watercolor. The artist leaves no doubt about the character of his subject, the most detested prince of the realm.

Thomas Rowlandson:
Blood Royal, c. 1802

Blood Royal—

149

On soft summer nights Londoners thronged Vauxhall to listen to concerts and stroll along brightly illuminated paths. In this Rowlandson drawing, a crowd has gathered for a solo performance by a Mrs. Weichsel. In the supper box at lower left the portly Dr. Johnson prepares to dine, while to his right the writer Oliver Goldsmith has already started to wolf his meal; nearby, Johnson's devoted biographer Boswell holds a bowl. Rowlandson placed

Thomas Rowlandson: *Vauxhall Gardens*, c. 1784

many renowned figures in the crowd, including the Prince of Wales *(right center)*, who engages in a tête-à-tête with his first major heart interest, the lovely actress Perdita Robinson, while her diminutive elderly escort fumes. The wanton ways at Vauxhall shocked many foreigners. One noted with alarm the manner in which bold women and their pimps pushed their way into booths "and in the most shameless manner importuned . . . for wine."

A special gusto marked the English country fairs. Farmers free of their arduous labors, townsfolk in holiday silks and ruffles, and local squires with their ladies flocked to these occasions. As Rowlandson records in this exuberant watercolor, sideshows with tumblers, actors and a giant were prime attractions, but the fairs also offered visitors new ways to show off. A prize was awarded to the man who could leap over the most horses

Thomas Rowlandson: *Fairlop Fair (The Fair)*, date unknown

placed side by side, or catch a running pig by its greased tail, or hold a grin the longest while thrusting his head through an old horse collar. Wheelbarrow races with blindfolded contestants provided rowdy frolic, and drinking and eating contests were gleefully joined. Amid these pleasures, however, one competition was the favorite: the unremitting battle of the sexes, in which winners and losers were often indistinguishable.

High Adventure in the Hinterlands

A passion for travel swept England in the late 18th Century. The grand tour of the Continent was considered a must for young men of means, and less ambitious trips to various corners of the British Isles were also the rage. Books on travel proliferated. Countless Englishmen who had trekked to Salisbury, Land's End or Wales felt constrained to commit their experiences to paper—usually in painful detail. Part of this eagerness to explore the homeland was attributable to improved highways and more comfortable coaches, part to a growing appreciation of Britain's natural beauties—an affinity that found artistic outlet in the great native school of landscape painting that flourished well into the 19th Century.

But when Rowlandson and his friend and fellow artist Henry Wigstead toured southern England around 1784, their purpose was simply to have a good time. To present-day travelers their itinerary seems modest indeed. From London they journeyed through Salisbury, by packet from Lymington to the Isle of Wight in the English Channel, back to Portsmouth Harbour and home to London. The jaunt covered less than 250 miles, but it took about 12 days to complete. Nevertheless it was the sort of excursion that could be translated into high—and humorous—adventure. Rowlandson was then in his mid-twenties, and on the brink of success as a quizzical observer of his times. Gifted with a deft pen, he sketched every aspect of the trip from the predawn rising required at the take-off (*below*) to a tourist's view of the interior of a British man-of-war anchored in Portsmouth Harbour (*pages 158-159*). Using the scenery as a mere backdrop, Rowlandson concerned himself with the people he met along the way. The result is a travel record of unusual charm, heightened by insights into contemporary British customs and enlivened by Rowlandson's own captions.

Sir. Sir. Sir. its past 4 O Clock.

MR. ROWLANDSON'S OLD HOUSEKEEPER CALLING HIM UP ON THE MORNING WE SET OFF.

MR. WIGSTEAD TAKING LEAVE OF HIS HOME AND FAMILY—THE START.

THE DELAY—OR ACCIDENT, AT POPHAM LANE—ONE O'CLOCK.

155

COFFEE HOUSE IN SALISBURY MARKET PLACE.

SHIPPING OXEN ON BOARD THE ISLE OF WIGHT PACKET.

156

THE PRETTY HOSTESS, AND ROWLANDSON—WITH THE EXTRAVAGANT BILL, AND WIGSTEAD.

THE QUARTER-DECK OF THE VESSEL WHICH CARRIED US TO THE NEEDLES—THE WIND BLOWING HARD.

COWES HARBOUR IN THE ISLE OF WIGHT.

GOING ON BOARD THE "HECTOR," OF 74 GUNS, LYING IN PORTSMOUTH HARBOUR.

MIDDLE DECK OF THE "HECTOR," MAN-OF-WAR.

Engravings from *The Anatomy of the Horse*, 1766

The average English country gentleman regarded his horses with almost as much concern as his family. They were usually an integral feature of sporting pictures of country life, and a favored animal sometimes had its portrait displayed in the owner's trophy room. Nor was this affection limited to a man's own stable; paintings, prints and sketches of famous thoroughbreds adorned more manor-house walls than did portraits of national heroes or the Royal Family. Despite the popularity of such art, most British painters of animals were mediocre. The exception was George Stubbs, who raised this very specialized kind of painting to a high level.

Stubbs believed that human beings were at their best when in the company of animals. In the paintings at right he reveals his deep-seated conviction in the unity of all God's creatures. Man and beast radiate a serenity and a natural harmony. As much a scientist as a painter, Stubbs undertook the most comprehensive study of the horse conceived up to that time. His monumental volume, *The Anatomy of the Horse*, shows and describes in intricate detail the structure of a horse from the inside out *(above)*, and is still respected as a classic in its field.

160

George Stubbs: *The Melbourne and Milbanke Families,* 1770

George Stubbs: *Phaeton with Cream Ponies and Stable-Lad,* c. 1785

Stubbs attacked his study of the horse with the zest and determination that were characteristic of his era. He read endlessly on the subject, but his real knowledge came from firsthand experience. In his isolated farmhouse in Lincolnshire he carefully dissected dozens of dead horses, detailing every bone, muscle and organ in copious drawings. Possessed of a strong back as well as a probing, empirical mind, Stubbs was said to be able to carry a dead horse upstairs to his dissecting rooms all by himself. Sharing Stubbs's odoriferous world of dead horses was his companion and assistant, Mary Spencer, reportedly an aunt or a niece, but probably his mistress. Whatever the

George Stubbs: *Brood Mares and Foals,* c. 1762

relationship, she must have been blessed with a sound constitution to cope with life at Lincolnshire.

Stubbs won an international reputation with the publication of his book. At the same time, his paintings of horses, such as the one shown above, secured his artistic fame. This uncompleted frieze, to which the artist never bothered to add his customary background of carefully detailed landscape, shows Stubbs at the peak of his talent. Working with meticulous precision, he arranged the horses to form a smoothly flowing arabesque in which each animal is equally important as an individual study and as part of a harmonious composition.

VIII

Tribute from a Rival

The most productive years of Gainsborough's life, and also his most creative, came when he had passed his 50th birthday and was fully established in London. By now he had become so adept at portrait painting and was getting such high prices that he could earn a lavish living in very little time. Except for his nephew and apprentice, Gainsborough Dupont, he employed no assistants to paint drapery and backgrounds as most other prominent painters did, but even without such help his speed was phenomenal. When he was in the mood he would complete a couple of full-length portraits in a few weeks and collect 160 guineas for each. Then he could relax with his musical or theatrical friends and their diverting women, or lounge in Christie's auction rooms. There he studied the paintings, especially the old masters, that were put up for sale and made mental notes about them for reference in his own work. He was a great crony of James Christie's, who valued the artist's expert opinion and always made him welcome. Sometimes Gainsborough was joined by his actor friend David Garrick, and together they joked with the customers. Christie often remarked that the lively humor of the famous pair added 15 per cent to his commission on a sale.

But most of the free time that financial success allowed Gainsborough he invested in various artistic experiments. In some he used media new to him. He tried painting in watercolor, then adding a coat of varnish to simulate the effect of thinly laid oil paint. He also painted seascapes—although he had no previous interest in the sea—and did them extraordinarily well, displaying a surprisingly accurate knowledge of ships, sails and waves. The eminent man of letters Horace Walpole admired two of these tours de force in the Royal Academy's exhibition of 1781 and remarked that they appeared "so free and natural that one steps back for fear of being splashed."

Perhaps Gainsborough's most radical experiment was painting on glass with transparent colors. To show off the resulting scenes—only about a foot square—he mounted them in a wooden light box that contained three candles to light them from the rear, somewhat like lantern slides. Ten of his transparencies are now in the Victoria and Albert Museum in

One of Gainsborough's last wishes was that this self-portrait be the only likeness of him publicized after his death. Begun the year before, probably as a gift for a friend, the painting became his statement of how he wished to be remembered. His daughter Margaret presented it to the Royal Academy, where it hangs today.

Portrait of the Artist, c. 1787

Gainsborough's Peep Show

As an experiment with the effects of light on landscapes, Gainsborough devised the wooden box below, similar to a modern color-slide viewer. The spectator gazed through a lens (A) in the front of the box at scenes that Gainsborough had painted on glass. These were fitted into a holder (B) in the middle of the box and lighted from behind by candles. Six of the 10 extant slides he painted are shown here. Gainsborough often diverted his friends with an evening of peep-show exhibitions.

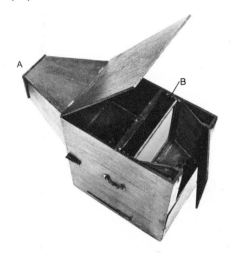

Woodland scene

Moonlit cottage

London, set into the wall of a dim corridor where the light coming through them gives a gay and lively effect. They show cattle nearing a stream in which the colors of sunset are brightly reflected, a river with white-water rapids, and ships approaching a harbor against a brilliant sky. The most impressive of these paintings on glass depicts a small cottage at late dusk with the last traces of sunset glowing behind it and a cozy, friendly light streaming from its window and door. In this small picture, done in an unusual and difficult medium, Gainsborough makes a very humble home seem a happy refuge from a dark and hostile world.

The experiment closest to Gainsborough's heart, however, was the development of landscapes in which figures of human beings—who had been only incidental in his earlier landscapes—became as important as the scenery in which they were set. Gainsborough, perhaps unique among painters in his remarkable command of both landscape and portraiture, combined the two kinds of painting with great success and in several different ways.

One combination is illustrated by the charming scene called *The Mall in St. James's Park,* in which a dozen-odd elegant ladies in all their finery drift along a London promenade while their little dogs prance among them. The picture is a full-fledged landscape with carefully stage-managed foliage and gnarled, nearly dead trees resembling those that Gainsborough had painted when he was a young man in Suffolk. Yet the ladies, in their gorgeous clothes, are integral parts of the composition, and although small they are also individuals; their faces, no more than one and a half inches high, are as perfectly and delicately painted as miniatures. The whole scene is so wonderfully alive that Walpole described it as being "all a flutter, like a lady's fan." It could only be the work of a master landscape painter who was also a master portraitist.

In another painting, one of Gainsborough's so-called "fancy pictures"—landscapes with figures in which he let his fancy roam freely and poetically—the artist used a very different combination. The single human figure in *Girl with Pigs* is no lady of fashion but a little sad-faced peasant girl, barefoot and ragged, sitting on a cottage step and watching three young pigs eating from a dish. Nor did Gainsborough portray her in the same small scale as his strollers in *The Mall.* Instead, her figure, placed prominently in the foreground, dominates the scene.

The pigs in the picture were actually brought into the artist's studio. One of Gainsborough's musical friends, William Parke, wrote that "when this work was in progress I have seen at his house in Pall Mall the three little pigs (who did not in the common phrase sit for their likenesses) gambolling about his painting room, whilst he at his easel was catching an attitude or a leer from them."

In painting *Girl with Pigs,* Gainsborough demonstrated something more than his superb skill in blending portraiture and the world of nature. He also revealed the love and kinship he felt for humble people, while his tender treatment of the little girl clearly betrays his delight in the beauty of children. The model's identity is not known. She was probably a street urchin whom Gainsborough persuaded to pose, or she may even have been the daughter of a real peasant. In any case the hours he spent with this pretty, unsophisticated child must have compensated for the boredom of glorifying many tedious duchesses.

Girl with Pigs was shown at the Royal Academy in 1782 and was the hit of the exhibition. It was extravagantly praised by the critics and was bought by the Academy's president, Sir Joshua Reynolds himself, who was so enthusiastic about the painting that he paid Gainsborough 40 guineas more than its listed price of 60. Editor Henry Bate, "The Fighting Parson," wrote in his *Morning Herald* that Sir Joshua, "whose liberality is equal to his genius, the moment he saw this picture sent to know the price, and purchased it, sending a hundred guineas with half as many elegant compliments on the work of the artist, who is said to have written back 'that it could not fail to afford him the highest satisfaction that he had brought his pigs to so fair a market.' "

Sir Joshua considered the picture the best that Gainsborough had ever painted or might ever paint, but he suggested that the face of the girl could have been made more beautiful. He probably meant more "ideal," like his own classicized faces. Gainsborough, always independent, did not follow his advice—if he ever heard it. For the rest of his life he portrayed his peasants and their children as individuals as full of character as their social betters, and he often gave the children the heart-rending sadness that only the very young can show.

Distant hills

In depicting these lowly people as very human beings, Gainsborough was in accord with a new spirit that was beginning to reshape the world. The late 18th Century was not only the heyday of aristocracy at its gaudiest; it was also a time when poets and philosophers increasingly eulogized simplicity and praised the virtues of the common man. This feeling provided much of the force behind the American War of Independence and the much bloodier French Revolution of 1789. Britain had no violent uprising, but there was a revolution in thought. The lower classes came to be idealized instead of being vilified as brutes and dolts, as had been the earlier custom.

Broad valley

Because of the late-18th Century state of mind, these pictures, so obviously sympathetic to a downtrodden class, were enormously admired by London society and were usually bought at high prices by the same landowning noblemen who were responsible for the poverty of the peasants. Perhaps Gainsborough never noticed this contradiction. He continued to paint fashionable portraits, but at a slower pace, while devoting most of his time and enthusiasm to "fancy pictures" and more realistic scenes featuring poor country people. Although moralizing was not Gainsborough's nature, one of these, *The Beggars*, seems almost a sermon on the contrast of wealth and poverty. It shows a miserable country woman with her five small children standing at the door of an elegant manor house while a servant pours food into a hat held by her oldest son. This picture somehow received the title of *Charity Relieving Distress*, but Gainsborough surely did not mean it as praise for the prosperous.

The Thames

When the Royal Academy was planning its exhibition of 1783, Gainsborough's relations with its officials seemed ideal, from his point of view at least. For that year's exhibition he sent 26 pictures, 15 of which were bust-length portraits of members of the Royal Family. Accompanying

River scene

them was a note for the Academy's governing council, which included not only President Reynolds but many other leading painters: "Mr. Gainsborough presents his compliments to the Gentlemen appointed to hang the pictures at the Royal Academy: and begs leave to *hint* to them that if the Royal Family, which he has sent for this Exhibition *(being smaller than three-quarters)* are hung above the line along with full-lengths, he never more, whilst he breaths, will send another picture to the Exhibition. This he swears by God."

A less belligerent note to the secretary of the Academy explained how he wanted the royal portraits placed and enclosed a sketch showing all 15 of them arranged frame to frame in three rows of five each with the King at the upper left-hand corner. This request, which may have been prompted by the court, was carried out exactly as Gainsborough stipulated. The 15 portraits, fitted together as a unit, were displayed directly opposite the entrance of the exhibition gallery, where they were sure to be the first things seen by the crowds that crammed the hall almost to the point of suffocation.

The paintings were not universally praised. Except for the Queen, the family of George III had not stimulated Gainsborough to his best efforts, and the satirist and poet Peter Pindar pretended to doubt that Gainsborough painted them at all: "For let me perish if I think them thine." Some critics hinted darkly that the arrangement of the pictures was an expression of the court's notoriously bad taste. The *St. James's Chronicle* commented: "We can only say that these pictures are prettily painted, but the various positions of the faces are by no means well chosen. The whole, even to the method of framing them, is a childish conceit and by no means worthy of Mr. Gainsborough. We suppose, therefore, that it had another origin."

Before the exhibition was over, resentment had once again boiled up between the touchy Gainsborough and the Academy's bureaucrats. Both sides had reason for rancor. The hanging committee was antagonized by the fact that Gainsborough had dictated the placement of his pictures and got away with it. Perhaps in retaliation the committee had hung his portrait of Lady Horatia Waldegrave—daughter of the Lady Waldegrave whose portrait may have triggered Gainsborough's first quarrel with the Academy in 1772—against a boarded-up fireplace where it would be brushed by the skirts of women visitors crowding to look at miniatures above the mantel. The scandal of "the lady in the fireplace" made a great noise in the newspapers, and Gainsborough was reported to be so angry that he tried to withdraw all his pictures and was barely persuaded not to do so.

For the exhibition of 1784 he prepared (perhaps with misgivings) 18 pictures, including a full-length group portrait of the three eldest daughters of King George III. This ambitious but slightly vapid picture was painted to fill a particular place in Carlton House, the residence of the Prince of Wales, where a frame had already been built into a wall to receive it. Since Gainsborough knew what the lighting there would be, he had painted the picture accordingly and he hated to think how bleak the Princesses would look if the Academy hung them "on the line," with

Now a yellowed document preserved in the archives of the Royal Academy, this sheet of paper set in motion the events that put Gainsborough at odds with the Academy's judges. It is the artist's sketch of eight portraits he planned to show at the Academy's exhibition in 1784. Under each picture he identified the sitters, and explained at the left that the portrait of the Royal Princesses *(upper left-hand corner)* had to be shown to Their Majesties before it could be sent on to the Academy. But because of a dispute over how this portrait should be hung, Gainsborough withdrew all his pictures from the exhibit for that year, and refused to show at the Academy again.

ROYAL ACADEMY OF ARTS, LONDON

their toes eight feet above the floor. When he asked that the portrait be placed lower, the hanging committee refused, and the matter was referred to the council. This time the Academy did not yield and neither did Gainsborough. His letter to the Academy was elaborately polite but final: "Mr. Gainsborough's compliments to the Gentlemen of the Committee, and begs pardon for giving them so much trouble, but as he has painted the Picture of the Princesses, in so tender a light, that notwithstanding he approves very much of the established Line for strong effects, he cannot possibly consent to have it placed higher than five feet & a half, because the likenesses & Work of the Picture will not be seen any higher; therefore at a word, he will not trouble the Gentlemen against their Inclination, but will beg the rest of his pictures back again."

The secession of Gainsborough from the Academy was the sensation of London society. Recriminations flew thick and fast, and Sir Joshua was rumored to be dusting off old pictures to fill the gaps left by his rival's departure. In midsummer of 1784, after the excitement had quieted down, Gainsborough opened his own exhibition room at Schomberg House, where there was plenty of space for all the pictures he cared to show. The timing was poor; the London social season had ended and most of the fashionable people had left the city, but gradually the gallery gained popularity. He sold many pictures off its walls and apparently did not suffer from the loss of the Academy as a showcase. He continued to paint the Royal Family and had more nonroyal portrait work than he could handle. Without much drudgery he was earning all the money that even his carefree hand could spend.

During the spring and early summer of 1787 Gainsborough was preoccupied with the "fancy picture" that he believed would be his best work. It shows a tattered woodman sheltering under a tree in the path of an approaching storm, his glance turned toward the angry sky; a bundle of branches he has cut in the forest lies behind him, and the mongrel dog at his feet is startled by a clap of thunder. The painting is indeed extraordinary, for it represents the artist's highest expression of sympathy for the humble—the woodman's face is pathetic, but it is also Christlike in its dignity and purity.

Even before it was finished, *The Woodman* was famous. While Gainsborough was adding the final touches, editor Bate hailed it in the *Morning Herald* and described how it came to be painted: "This wonderful memorial of genius is a portrait, the original being a poor smith worn out by labour, and now a pensioner upon accidental charity. Mr. Gainsborough was struck with his careworn aspect and took him home; he enabled the needy wanderer by his generosity to live—and made him immortal by his art." When King George saw the painting he called it "a masterpiece" and for a while it was widely rumored that he would buy it. Finally it was sold to the Earl of Gainsborough (no relative of the artist) for the princely sum of 500 guineas. *The Woodman* was destroyed by fire in 1810, but Gainsborough had made a smaller copy *(page 184)* in oils to be reproduced as an engraving, and this survives to give a good idea of what the original looked like.

At the start of 1788, Gainsborough was 60 years old and at the peak of his talent. He had just finished an elegant portrait of Lady Petrie, niece of the Duke of Norfolk, and had started one of her brother, when he felt a premonition of death and asked his friend Sheridan, the playwright, to promise to come to his funeral. Sheridan agreed, and all seemed well for a time. But not long after, while attending a session of the trial of Warren Hastings, the former Governor General of India, for misconduct in office—a *cause célèbre* that fascinated all London—Gainsborough felt a chill and noticed a spot on the back of his neck that seemed uncommonly cold. A doctor told him it was a swollen gland, but it proved to be cancer, and fatal.

During his last illness, Gainsborough continued to paint, busying himself with little landscapes as his strength slowly failed. Some days before the end he wrote to Reynolds, whom he continued to hold in high regard despite his secession from the Academy in 1784: "The extreme affection which I am informed of by a Friend which Sir Joshua has expresed induces me to beg a last favor, which is to come once under my Roof and look at my things, my woodman you never saw, if what I ask now is not disagreeable to you. I can from a sincere Heart say that I always admired and sincerely loved Sir Joshua Reynolds."

When Sir Joshua came to Schomberg House, Gainsborough rallied enough to show many unfinished paintings that were brought to his bedside, and even expressed the hope that he would recover and complete them. But on August 2, 1788, he died. According to his fellow music lover and longtime friend William Jackson, his last whispered words were: "We are all going to Heaven, and Van Dyck is of the company."

Reynolds gave a moving account of his final meeting with his great rival. "I cannot prevail on myself," he said, "to suppress that I was not connected with him by any habits of familiarity; if any little jealousies had subsisted between us, they were forgotten, in those moments of sincerity; he turned to me as one, who was engrossed by the same pursuits, and who deserved his good opinion, by being sensible of his excellence. Without entering into a detail of what passed at this last interview, the impression of it upon my mind was, that his regret at losing life, was principally the regret of leaving his art; and more especially as he now began, he said, to see what his deficiencies were."

These sentences are contained in Sir Joshua's 14th Discourse to the Royal Academy, which he delivered four months after Gainsborough's death (four years before his own) and which he devoted entirely to an analysis of Gainsborough's art. He was deeply appreciative but also somewhat envious in a gentlemanly way, and not a little baffled. "We have lately lost Mr. Gainsborough," said Sir Joshua, "one of the greatest ornaments of our Academy . . . If ever this nation should produce genius sufficient to acquire to us the honorable distinction of an English school, the name of Gainsborough will be transmitted to posterity, in the history of the art, among the very first of that rising name."

Accurately, though probably through hearsay, he sketched Gainsborough's character and described "some of the customs and habits of this extraordinary man. . . . Among others he had a habit of continually remarking, to those who happened to be about him, whatever peculiarity

Gainsborough felt the first symptom of the cancer that subsequently killed him while attending the sensational trial of Warren Hastings in crowded Westminster Hall *(above)*. A former Governor General of India, Hastings was accused of official misconduct on vindictive charges that played on a rising popular concern with the welfare of subject peoples. In fact, Hastings had been an able, just and honest administrator and he was cleared of all wrongdoing in a parliamentary trial that lasted more than seven years and attracted huge crowds.

of countenance, whatever accidental combination of figures, or happy effects of light and shadow, occurred in prospects, in the sky, in walking the streets, or in company." Reynolds talked of Gainsborough's custom of painting by candlelight, of bringing unusual people and even animals into his studio to serve as models, and of his composing landscapes out of a collection of mosses, weeds and stones. Sir Joshua was not sure that these habits were proper; they were certainly not in accordance with the rules and disciplines that he tried to follow in his own work. But he freely admitted that they often led Gainsborough to extraordinary triumphs. He dwelt long on what he felt was his rival's lack of finish—"those odd scratches and marks, which, on close examination, are so observable in Gainsborough's pictures, and which even to experienced painters appear rather the effect of accident than design; this chaos; this uncouth and shapeless appearance, by a kind of magic, at a certain distance assumes form, and all the parts seem to drop into their proper places; so that we can hardly refuse acknowledging the full effect of diligence, under the appearance of chance and hasty negligence."

After praising Gainsborough's talent for capturing likenesses, his facility and deft handling of color, Sir Joshua urged the Academy's students not to try to follow Gainsborough along what seemed to Reynolds an unorthodox path. They must observe, he warned, "the great rules and principles of the art, as they are collected from the full body of the best general practice."

The 14th Discourse proved that Reynolds could rise above any jealousies he may have felt in the past. But it also revealed the perplexity of a talented man of reason confronted face to face by an authentic but intuitive genius.

This miniature portrait was painted by Johann Zoffany just three years before Gainsborough's death. His sensitive features reflect the strains that long taxed his high-strung temperament. Concern for his two daughters, whose emotional instability became increasingly evident over the years, and the aggravations of his unhappy marriage had darkened his personal life. But he had achieved wide recognition and great success, and an air of confidence born of attainment distinguishes his handsome face.
GAINSBOROUGH'S HOUSE SOCIETY, SUDBURY

Reynolds' advice to art students not to follow Gainsborough was sound; Gainsborough was much too original and individual to serve as a model. In portraiture, at least, most of Britain's younger painters would pursue the tradition established by Reynolds. In landscape painting, however, and in his sympathetic portrayal of the common people, Gainsborough's influence was great. His "fancy pictures" and landscapes were frequently copied and imitated and were immensely popular when reproduced as engravings. Although British artists did not abandon the old tradition of traveling abroad in search of more spectacular or romantic vistas and scenes, a numerous school of painters followed his lead in painting the relatively modest beauties of British scenery. John Constable, the great British landscape painter who was most influenced by Gainsborough, summed up the artist's spirit in one of his lectures: "The landscape of Gainsborough is soothing, tender, and affecting. The stillness of noon, the depths of twilight, and the dews and pearls of the morning, are all to be found on the canvases of this most benevolent and kind-hearted man. On looking at them, we find tears in our eyes, and know not what brings them. The lonely haunts of the solitary shepherd, the return of the rustic with his bill and bundle of wood, the darksome lane or dell, the sweet little cottage girl at the spring with her pitcher, were the things he delighted to paint, and which he painted with an exquisite refinement, yet not a refinement beyond nature."

Labors of Love

Gainsborough loved the Suffolk countryside where he and his eight brothers and sisters had romped as children and where, as a youth, he had wandered through the fields on sketching expeditions. There was, says a biographer, "not a picturesque clump of trees, nor even a single tree of any beauty, no, nor hedge-row, stem, or post" in his home that he did not know by heart. It was always to the countryside that he dreamed of returning.

As his success as a portraitist took him from provincial Ipswich to the resort of Bath and finally to the teeming city of London, Gainsborough grew increasingly sentimental about the scenes of his boyhood. Portraits demanded much of his effort, but some time was always reserved for landscapes. He did hundreds of them. Some were sold; many more he gave to his friends or stacked away in closets.

Having to rely on memory rather than sketching tours, the busy artist laid out miniature forests on a tabletop, with stalks of broccoli for trees. Dolls dressed in scraps of cloth served as models for the small human figures he put into his earlier landscapes simply to establish scale or to divert the viewer's eye. But in time his landscapes began to include sweet-faced farm children and lowly field hands, prominently featured and portrayed with care and warmth. Gainsborough died believing that his finest achievement was his loving depiction of England's countryside and the virtuous folk who peopled it.

Landscapes by Dutch artists decorated many homes in Gainsborough's native Suffolk, a coastal county that traded with Holland. He based this early sketch on a painting by Jacob van Ruisdael of Haarlem, in which dark tree shade is juxtaposed with pools of bright sunshine.

La Forêt (after Ruisdael), c. 1748

173

A stream of shimmering clear water draws the eye into this charcoal sketch; a sparsely branched tree marks the middle distance. Traces of human life are few: in the background a castle on the cliff, in the foreground a man punting his shallow-draft boat.

Gainsborough created this charming scene, more from imagination than memory, during an interlude in his portrait work at Bath in the 1760s. The balance and perspective of the composition amply satisfied the artistic conventions of his time. To these Gainsborough added what was to become his hallmark as a landscapist, a romantic and casual quality that led one lady to dub such sketches Gainsborough's "moppings." He achieved this seemingly unstudied effect by using a bit of sponge tied to a stick as a pencil to create shadows and holding a lump of chalk in a pair of tongs to lay in the highlights.

Landscape, c. 1766-1774

The Boy in the Cart, c. 1760-1770

The country lad in the old wooden cart above might well be Gainsborough's remembrance of himself, in momentary nostalgia for the rutted roads and leafy lanes of Suffolk. This quick drawing conveys a lazy mood of boyhood just as convincingly as Gainsborough's painstaking portraits personify elegance.

The artist roughed out many such drawings without any thought of selling them, but they were no idle doodlings. Ideas from his early sketches often cropped up later in finished paintings; the rickety cart reappears (with livelier passengers and team) in *The Harvest Waggon (page 180),* one of Gainsborough's masterpieces in oil.

Through these sketches, too, Gainsborough evinced his deepening interest in country people. From shadowy figures of little importance they develop into individuals, like the boy in the cart, who set a mood. And finally they become significant subjects in their own right, as in *A Cottage Girl with Dog and Pitcher (right),* produced in Gainsborough's last decade.

By then he seems to have discovered that it was the people, even more than the land and sky, that he loved about the countryside. This barefooted girl on her way to the well he painted with fatherly tenderness. A critic carped about "sentimental pensiveness . . . which is only an idea existing in the painter's mind." But Gainsborough *was* sentimental—and painted what he felt.

A Cottage Girl with Dog and Pitcher, 1785

177

The Wood Gatherers (Cottage Children), 1787

A young woman, weary from gathering mushrooms, has dozed off against a rustic fence. Sunshine filters through the leaves of an old elm to play on the fair skin of her cheek and shoulder. Her straw hat, slipped back, seems to suggest a halo. Upon this scene comes a lad from the hayfields. He is struck by the girl's beauty and leans so gently against the fence to gaze at her that her terrier, though eying him curiously, does not bark and awaken its mistress.

Of such idealized pastorals did Gainsborough spin what he called his "fancy pictures." The *Haymaker and the Sleeping Girl (right)* was thought by one of his biographers to be based on a tale in Boccaccio's *Decameron*, but Gainsborough was not really concerned with literary allusions. Rather, he gloried in unabashed sentimentality.

In *The Wood Gatherers (top right)* and *The Cottage Door (far right)*, Gainsborough's figures wear the ragged clothes of poverty—the mothers resemble patient, long-suffering Madonnas—suggesting that the artist was keenly aware of the injustices that befell the common folk in English society. Still, he was never moved to use his art as propaganda or preachment. He had no desire to portray the poor in the same light as Hogarth's wretched Gin Lane Londoners. But Gainsborough did show, unmistakably, that nature was kinder to these cottage people than were their fellow men.

Haymaker and the Sleeping Girl (The Mushroom Girl), c. 1788

The Cottage Door, c. 1780

The Harvest Waggon, exhibited c. 1767; later version (not shown here) painted 1784-1785

One part of a Picture," Gainsborough said, "ought to be like the first part of a Tune; that you can guess what follows, and that makes the second part of the Tune." He very often liked to show a road running through his landscape paintings, in much the same way a melodic line runs through a piece of music: it might submerge or disappear intermittently, but its effect was to give his work a unity, a sense of beginning, middle and end.

As the viewer's eye travels with the cart or the riders along the two roads on these pages, it passes through a density of picturesque detail. One critic, speaking of the scene above, enumerated the "overhung and broken banks, the furze bushes and tussocks, the tufts of grass and broad burdock leaves, even the broken tracks of the cart,

Mountain Landscape with Peasants Crossing Bridge, c. 1785

the large knots and protuberances of the aging tree, the mosses on its bark, and the blackness of decayed wood." It is such details as these that give both pictures an astonishing textural quality.

In the *Mountain Landscape* such evocations of nature dominate the picture. In *The Harvest Waggon* they are subordinated to a group of colorful homebound country people. Gainsborough, who admired Rubens, borrowed the composition of the scene's focal point—the group at the wagon *(detail, following pages)*—from the Flemish artist's *Descent from the Cross* at Antwerp Cathedral. The lad leaning over the wheel to help his girl friend climb into the wagon is caught at the same angle as one of the men lowering Christ's body in Rubens' masterpiece.

The Woodman, c. 1787-1788

Very near the end of life, Gainsborough painted his last great "fancy picture," a poetic portrait of a countryman caught beneath a darkening, thunderous sky and turning his eyes heavenward. The image must have had special poignancy for the artist. It was one that he particularly wished Joshua Reynolds to see when he invited his old friendly rival to pay a call in July 1788. By then he was already confined to bed, dying of cancer.

Gainsborough's original painting of *The Woodman* was more than seven and a half feet high and about five feet wide. It was sold shortly after his death, and was destroyed in a fire in 1810. Gainsborough, however, had made another version of the painting—a small copy only two feet high—which he had evidently intended as a model for an engraver who was to make a print of the work. The picture at the left is the small *Woodman,* reproduced here in color for the first time. The artist's nephew, Gainsborough Dupont, may have had a hand in finishing it, but the painting nevertheless stands as a landmark in the work of a master. Filled with emotion —even the dog is animated with fear—the picture powerfully conveys the communion between man and nature. It was Gainsborough's last testament.

Chronology: Artists of Gainsborough's Era

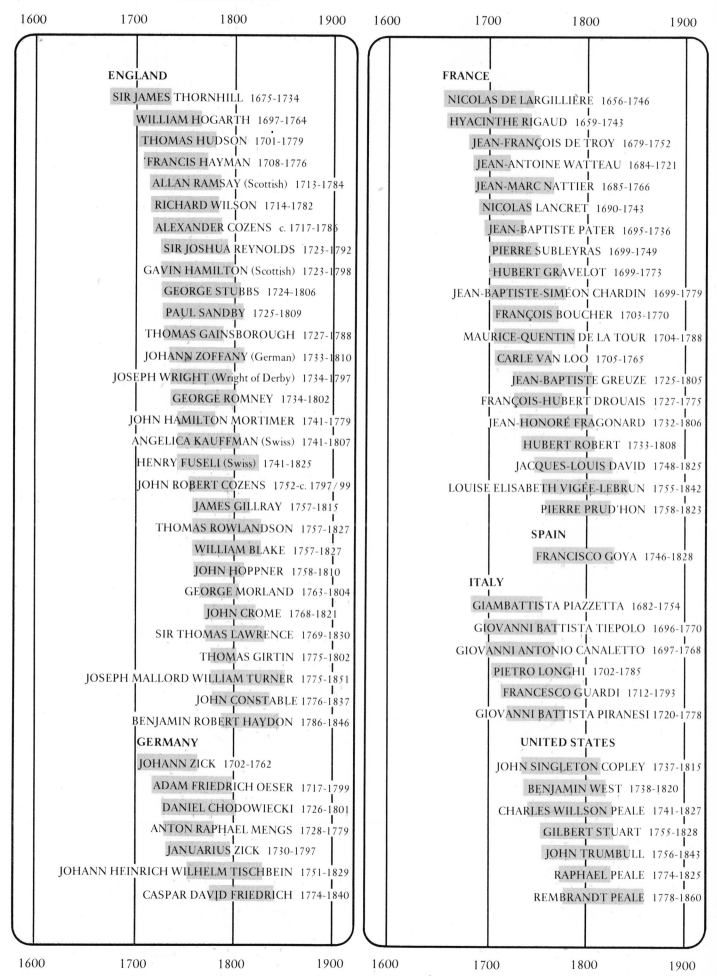

1600	1700	1800	1900

ENGLAND

SIR JAMES THORNHILL 1675-1734
WILLIAM HOGARTH 1697-1764
THOMAS HUDSON 1701-1779
FRANCIS HAYMAN 1708-1776
ALLAN RAMSAY (Scottish) 1713-1784
RICHARD WILSON 1714-1782
ALEXANDER COZENS c. 1717-1786
SIR JOSHUA REYNOLDS 1723-1792
GAVIN HAMILTON (Scottish) 1723-1798
GEORGE STUBBS 1724-1806
PAUL SANDBY 1725-1809
THOMAS GAINSBOROUGH 1727-1788
JOHANN ZOFFANY (German) 1733-1810
JOSEPH WRIGHT (Wright of Derby) 1734-1797
GEORGE ROMNEY 1734-1802
JOHN HAMILTON MORTIMER 1741-1779
ANGELICA KAUFFMAN (Swiss) 1741-1807
HENRY FUSELI (Swiss) 1741-1825
JOHN ROBERT COZENS 1752-c. 1797/99
JAMES GILLRAY 1757-1815
THOMAS ROWLANDSON 1757-1827
WILLIAM BLAKE 1757-1827
JOHN HOPPNER 1758-1810
GEORGE MORLAND 1763-1804
JOHN CROME 1768-1821
SIR THOMAS LAWRENCE 1769-1830
THOMAS GIRTIN 1775-1802
JOSEPH MALLORD WILLIAM TURNER 1775-1851
JOHN CONSTABLE 1776-1837
BENJAMIN ROBERT HAYDON 1786-1846

GERMANY

JOHANN ZICK 1702-1762
ADAM FRIEDRICH OESER 1717-1799
DANIEL CHODOWIECKI 1726-1801
ANTON RAPHAEL MENGS 1728-1779
JANUARIUS ZICK 1730-1797
JOHANN HEINRICH WILHELM TISCHBEIN 1751-1829
CASPAR DAVID FRIEDRICH 1774-1840

1600	1700	1800	1900

FRANCE

NICOLAS DE LARGILLIÈRE 1656-1746
HYACINTHE RIGAUD 1659-1743
JEAN-FRANÇOIS DE TROY 1679-1752
JEAN-ANTOINE WATTEAU 1684-1721
JEAN-MARC NATTIER 1685-1766
NICOLAS LANCRET 1690-1743
JEAN-BAPTISTE PATER 1695-1736
PIERRE SUBLEYRAS 1699-1749
HUBERT GRAVELOT 1699-1773
JEAN-BAPTISTE-SIMÉON CHARDIN 1699-1779
FRANÇOIS BOUCHER 1703-1770
MAURICE-QUENTIN DE LA TOUR 1704-1788
CARLE VAN LOO 1705-1765
JEAN-BAPTISTE GREUZE 1725-1805
FRANÇOIS-HUBERT DROUAIS 1727-1775
JEAN-HONORÉ FRAGONARD 1732-1806
HUBERT ROBERT 1733-1808
JACQUES-LOUIS DAVID 1748-1825
LOUISE ELISABETH VIGÉE-LEBRUN 1755-1842
PIERRE PRUD'HON 1758-1823

SPAIN

FRANCISCO GOYA 1746-1828

ITALY

GIAMBATTISTA PIAZZETTA 1682-1754
GIOVANNI BATTISTA TIEPOLO 1696-1770
GIOVANNI ANTONIO CANALETTO 1697-1768
PIETRO LONGHI 1702-1785
FRANCESCO GUARDI 1712-1793
GIOVANNI BATTISTA PIRANESI 1720-1778

UNITED STATES

JOHN SINGLETON COPLEY 1737-1815
BENJAMIN WEST 1738-1820
CHARLES WILLSON PEALE 1741-1827
GILBERT STUART 1755-1828
JOHN TRUMBULL 1756-1843
RAPHAEL PEALE 1774-1825
REMBRANDT PEALE 1778-1860

1600	1700	1800	1900

Gainsborough's predecessors, contemporaries and successors are grouped chronologically according to country. The bands correspond to the life spans of the artists.

Bibliography *Available in paperback.

GAINSBOROUGH—HIS LIFE AND WORK

Fulcher, George Williams, *The Letters of Thomas Gainsborough, R.A.* Longman, Brown, Green, Longman, 1856.

Gower, Lord Ronald Sutherland, *Thomas Gainsborough.* George Bell and Sons, London, 1903.

Roberts, Keith, *Gainsborough.** Knowledge Publications. Purnell & Sons Ltd., London, 1966.

Thicknesse, Philip, *A Sketch of the Life and Paintings of Thomas Gainsborough, Esq.* London, 1788.

Waterhouse, Ellis K., *Gainsborough.* Spring Books, London, 1966.

Whitley, William T., *Thomas Gainsborough.* John Murray, London, 1915.

Woodall, Mary:
Gainsborough's Landscape Drawings. Faber and Faber Ltd., London, 1939.
The Letters of Thomas Gainsborough. New York Graphic, 1963.
Thomas Gainsborough: His Life and Work. Chanticleer, 1949.

ART—HISTORICAL AND CULTURAL BACKGROUND

Baker, C. H. Collins, and Montague R. James, *British Painting.* Hale, 1934.

Boswell, James, *Boswell's Life of Samuel Johnson.* The Modern Library.

Burton, Elizabeth, *The Pageant of Georgian England.* Charles Scribner's, 1967.

Chippendale, Thomas, *The Gentleman and Cabinet-Maker's Director,* 3rd ed., R. W. Symonds, ed. Towse Publishing Co., 1938.

Darlington, W. A., *Sheridan.* Macmillan, 1933.

Fosca, François, *The Eighteenth Century: Watteau to Tiepolo,* trans. by Stuart Gilbert. Albert Skira, Geneva, 1952.

Gaunt, William, *A Concise History of English Painting.** Praeger, 1964.

Hepplewhite, A., and Co., *The Cabinet-Maker and Upholsterer's Guide.* Towse Publishing Co., 1942.

Hodgson and Eaton, *The Royal Academy and Its Members 1768-1830.* Scribner, 1905.

Hole, Christina, *English Home Life (1500-1800).* B. T. Batsford, Ltd., London, 1947.

Hutchinson, Sidney, *A History of the Royal Academy, 1768-1968.* Taplinger, 1968.

Jackson, William, *The Four Ages.* London, 1798.

Klingender, Francis D., *Art and the Industrial Revolution,* Arthur Elton, ed. Evelyn, Adams and Mackay, London, 1968.

Kronenberger, Louis, *Kings and Desperate Men.** Vintage, 1959.

Levey, Michael, *Rococo to Revolution: Major Trends in Eighteenth Century Painting.** Praeger, 1966.

Lunt, William Edward, *History of England,* 4th ed. Harper-Row, 1957.

Marshall, Dorothy, *English People in the Eighteenth Century.* Longmans, Green and Company, 1956.

Plumb, J. H., *The First Four Georges.* Macmillan, 1957.

Redman, Alvin, *The House of Hanover: From George I to Victoria.* Coward-McCann, Inc., 1960.

Sheppard, E. J., *Bath in the 18th Century.** Longmans, Green and Co., Ltd., London, 1966.

Sheraton, Thomas, *Sheraton's Complete Furniture Works.* Towse Publishing Co., 1946.

Sitwell, Edith, *Bath.* Faber and Faber, London, 1932.

Smith, R. A. L., *Bath.* B. T. Batsford, Ltd., London, 1948.

Trevelyan, G. M., *Illustrated English Social History,* Vol. 3, *18th Century.* McKay, 1949-1952.

ON OTHER PAINTERS

Antal, Frederick, *Hogarth and His Place in European Art.* Basic Books Inc., 1962.

Beckett, R. B., *John Constable's Correspondence.* Suffolk Records Society.

Bury, Adrian, ed., *Rowlandson Drawings.* Avalon Press, London, 1949.

Falk, Bernard, *Thomas Rowlandson: His Life and Work.* Beechhurst Press, 1952.

George, Dorothy M., *Hogarth to Cruikshank, Social Change in Graphic Satire.* Walker and Co., 1967.

Gombrich, E. H., "Reynolds's Theory and Practice of Imitation." *Burlington Magazine,* Vol. 80 (February 1942).

Greig, James, ed., *The Farington Diary.* 8 vols. Doran, 1925.

Hilles, Frederick W., ed., *Portraits by Sir Joshua Reynolds.* McGraw-Hill Book Co., Inc., 1952.

Hogarth, William, *The Analysis of Beauty,* Joseph Burke, ed. The Clarendon Press, Oxford, 1955.

Mitchell, Charles, "Three Phases of Reynolds's Method." *Burlington Magazine,* Vol. 80 (February 1942).

Paulson, Ronald, *Hogarth's Graphic Works,* Vol. 1, *Introduction and Catalogue;* Vol. 2, *The Engravings.* Yale University Press, 1965.

Reynolds, Sir Joshua, *Discourses to the Royal Academy.** Stephen O. Mitchell, ed. The Library of Liberal Arts. The Bobbs-Merrill Company, Inc., 1965.

Romantic Art in Britain: Paintings and Drawings 1760-1860. Philadelphia Museum of Art, 1968.

Sitwell, Sacheverell, *Conversation Pieces.* B. T. Batsford, London, 1936.

Smith, J. T., *Nollekens and His Times,* W. Whitten, ed. 2 vols. Turnstile Press, 1949.

Wark, Robert R., introduction and notes by, *Rowlandson's Drawings for a Tour in a Post Chaise.* The Huntington Library, San Marino, California, 1964.

Waterhouse, Ellis K.:
Painting in Britain 1530-1790. The Pelican History of Art. Penguin, 1953.
Three Decades of British Art 1740-1770. Jane Lectures for 1964. American Philosophical Society, Philadelphia, 1965.

Whitley, William T., *Artists and Their Friends in England, 1700-1799.* 2 vols. Hale, 1929.

Wilenski, Reginald Howard, *English Painting.* Hale, Cushman and Flint, 1937.

Acknowledgments

The author and editors of this book wish to thank the following: Frederick B. Adams Jr., Director, The Pierpont Morgan Library, New York; The Duke and Duchess of Bedford, Woburn Abbey, Bedford; Beverly Carter, Secretary, Paul Mellon Collection, Washington, D.C.; Cynthia Carter, Library Assistant, Photograph and Slide Library, The Metropolitan Museum of Art, New York; Bernice Davidson, Research Curator, The Frick Collection, New York; R. Sharpe France, County Archivist, Lancashire Record Office; Andrew Glaze, British Information Service, New York; Deane Hancock, Photograph Department, Museum of Fine Arts, Boston; Louise Houllier, Photographic Department, The Pierpont Morgan Library, New York; Elaine Hudson, Public Relations Department, The Metropolitan Museum of Art, New York; Colta Ives, Print Room, The Metropolitan Museum of Art, New York; David Johnson, Curator, Woburn Abbey, Bedford; Bard H. Langstaff, S. J. Shrubsole Corporation, New York; Karen McWhirter, Public Relations Department, The Metropolitan Museum of Art, New York; William W. Morrison, Assistant to the Director, National Gallery of Art, Washington, D.C.; The National Gallery, London; The Print Room of the British Museum, London; The Print Room of the Victoria and Albert Museum, London; Dowager Countess of Radnor, Wiltshire; Earl of Radnor, Wiltshire; The Earl Spencer, Northampton; Rowland Suddaby, Curator, Gainsborough's House Society, Sudbury; Susan Tuttle, Office of Public Information, National Gallery of Art, Washington, D.C.; Barbara A. Valentine, Secretary, Museum of Fine Arts, Boston; Ellis Waterhouse, Birmingham, England; Betty Zimmerman, Assistant Director, Cincinnati Art Museum, Cincinnati.

Picture Credits

Index

Numerals in italics indicate a picture of the subject mentioned. Unless otherwise identified, all listed art works are by Gainsborough. Dimensions are given in inches, unless otherwise indicated; height precedes width.

The typeface employed in this book is called Janson, after Anton Janson, the Dutch typefounder who popularized it in Leipzig in the late 17th Century. The face was first cut, however, by Nicholas Kis, a Hungarian working in Amsterdam in the 1680s.

xx

PRINTED IN U.S.A.